That's a Good One!

Avant® Leadership
Guide Series

That's a Good One!

Corporate Leadership With Humor

Bob Ross

Avant Books®
San Marcos, California

Library of Congress Cataloging-in-Publication Data
Ross, Bob
That's a good one! | corporate leadership with humor
Avant leadership guide series
1. Leadership.   2. Management.   3. Wit and humor.
I. Title.   II. Series.
HD57.7.R685 1991   658.4'092—dc20   90-27186

ISBN 0-932238-56-4

Avant Books®
Slawson Communications, Inc
San Marcos, CA 92069-1436

Printed in the United States

Interior Design by Sandra Mewshaw
Art by Estay Heustis

1 2 3 4 5 6 7 8 9 10

Dedication

To my parents for giving me the quality I treasure
most—my sense of humor.

Acknowledgments

I wish to express my appreciation to all those who helped in the preparation of this book. Newspaper articles, stories, and other related information given to me by my friends proved especially valuable in further developing the theory and practice espoused here. Gary Beals, Dan Conway, Chuck Gonzales, John Ross, Mark Sweat, and many others took the time to notice, clip, and send me supportive references, examples, and other material that proved invaluable. A special thanks to Carol Jackson, who did research and provided guidance and typing services; and my appreciation to Rebecca Smith, the manuscript editor.

Table of Contents

Introduction

In his early years, before becoming a renowned inventor, founding the Delco Company, and heading the General Motors Research Laboratory, Charles Kettering was foreman of a small gang of men setting telephone poles for a company in Ohio. T. A. Boyd, Kettering's biographer, wrote that one day a tramp came by looking for something to eat while the men were sitting in the shade eating lunch. Kettering took the man to a restaurant for a meal and then asked if he'd like a job so he could have plenty to eat.

Whether prompted by a sense of decency or by a sense of obligation to repay Kettering for the meal, the hobo accepted the offer. Kettering gave him some tools and left. On returning a little later, he found the man trying to dig a hole. The ground was underlain with shale, making hole digging a grueling task. However, with blistered hands and sweat streaming from his forehead, the man was trying. Wanting to encourage the inexperienced digger, Kettering had his best hole digger show him what a good hole looked like. It was round and smooth with straight walls. Then Kettering began digging a hole himself, telling the man what fun it was to dig a good hole—that the better the quality of the hole, the more fun the task.

Soon the hobo wanted to try his hand at digging the hole again. The results: The man stayed on, becoming not only the line gang's best hole digger but eventually its foreman. Sometime later, Kettering came across the former hobo. The man said to him, "You were the first person to tell me that work could be fun. If only years ago someone had taught me how much fun it is to work when a fellow does good work, I never would have become a bum." How one sees his or her job is reflected in the work produced—whether it's holes, an electronic component, or a satisfied customer.

I remember my father, as much as he dreaded it, getting up early every morning, *going into the shop*, and putting in his day's work. Because we all knew how much he hated his job, we saw his daily sacrifice as an act of love; and I recall how happy I felt for him when he finally retired after thirty years of drudgery. My perception of my father's unhappiness with work and my exposure to the news media's portrayal of work as being absolute toil did much to form my impression of the workplace as a very unpleasant but inevitable fact of life—like death, taxes and Rocky V.

I think that is the standard image instilled in most of us. We all have been indoctrinated to believe that work and play are opposites. If I were to give you a word association test of opposites, when I said "short" you would say "tall," "fat" would produce "skinny," and "work" would get me "play!"

This attitude is a holdover from the industrial era. It was, in fact, the essence of the Protestant ethic. But that notion belongs in a museum with the buggy whip. In the Information Age, getting the participation, commitment, and creativity of your work force is what management and leadership is all about. It's what separates the best companies from all the rest.

Think back in your own life to a moment of excellence. Recall something you did when you really excelled. It could have been an athletic event, a presentation you made, or a fine meal you prepared. The event itself doesn't matter, as long as it was one when you achieved excellence. Have you recaptured that event in your memory? Now let me tell you about it. I'll bet you worked hard but didn't consider it *hard work*. Wasn't that because you tackled the task with lots of enthusiasm, excitement, and exhilaration? Upon completion of the feat, you were overwhelmed with a sense of self-fulfillment. True? Of course it is; self-fulfillment is the source of all excellence! Have you ever heard of anyone achieving excellence through drudgery? I'll bet you can't think of even one example.

Why should you bother reading this book or taking the time to adopt fun and humor techniques? The answer can be found in one word: potential. Potential is reached when we become confused about the difference between work and recreation and find fulfillment in the achievement. How wonderful if we could make our hobbies our work. The wise recommend finding something that you would do for nothing—better yet, that you would pay someone to allow you to do—then making that your occupation. This is probably an unrealistic goal for some, but we can all come pretty close by trying to make work fun for our team and for ourselves. Humor creates fun, and fun leads to self-fulfillment. Potential is about self-fulfillment.

Does all this sound like a concept contrived by Pollyana? Or just another one of those passing trends? The principles discussed in this book will not only make sense and withstand the closest scrutiny, but they will be valid in the long run because they are based on certain aspects of human nature that will never change. There is nothing you can't do better if you're having fun!

If you're not having fun in your workplace nor encouraging fun among your workmates, maybe you just need a little encouragement. Please read on and I will take my best shot at giving you ways to make your workplace enjoyable. Not just because being an effective manager with a sense of humor is *nice*, not just because you and your fellow workers will see your jobs in a more positive light, not even because humor will lead to better health and a longer life—but because you'll do a better job!

Bob Ross

One

Humor in the Workplace

A sense of humor costs nothing,
but not having one can be very costly.

Are you living within a few miles of the place you were born, surrounded by family and old friends? If so, you probably know you're one of a vanishing breed. Americans are typically on the move from childhood through adulthood, frequently changing addresses, jobs, and mates. And household sizes are shrinking, with many now consisting of a childless couple, a single parent and child, or even a lone adult. Often our only meaningful interactions with people are in our workplace. Fellow employees are our friends, family, and neighbors. Thus we bring emotions to the job, and emotions are created on the job.

Today's leaders, taking these facts into consideration, must find effective ways of channeling emotions to decrease workers' job burnout and dropout while increasing productivity and profits. I believe the best way to accomplish this goal, and maybe the only way, is for management to create an environment where workers can have a good time while doing their jobs.

Some cling to the idea that employees aren't at work to enjoy themselves; certainly the company has no responsibility to see that they do. Employees are there to work, and that's what they are paid to do! These managers are right on one count: As an initial motivator, money is high on the list of reasons for taking a job. But what happens when money becomes the only incentive for remaining with a company? Imagined or real slights, stress, and dissatisfaction will lead just about all employees to resent their dependency on the money. What maintains employees' interest in their jobs is permission to be themselves, to grow, and to feel they have some control over their lives.

Now, how do you see your position? Would a sense of humor do more harm than good? Are you a front-line manager, a division head, a CEO—someone in a *serious* position? And how do you see yourself in relation to your work team? As a commander or a coach? To what extent do the members of the team consider you a part of it? Do you even have a team—or just a ragtag group of malcontents who come to work with the same level of enthusiasm with which they would face a rhinoceros stampede?

Now ask yourself, what do a close-knit family, a championship team, and a thriving business organization have in common? First and foremost, the members enjoy being together, laughing, playing, and having fun making things happen. And the best of the winning groups are those in which the leaders—parents, coaches, or managers—are considered members of the team.

You do not have to relinquish any of your status in the organization or go against company policy to be the leading member of your team. All you have to do is cultivate the one trait that will enhance all your other leadership attributes: a sense of humor.

Humor is an integral part of productive relationships. It is the oil that reduces friction and the glue that bonds. Perceptive managers, CEOs, business owners, and group leaders know that, with good humor and creative teamwork, the possibilities are unlimited. The old saying "The sky's the limit" has become obsolete. If this were not so, people would not have walked on the moon! The essence of good management is motivating people to work in concert, give their best, and enjoy themselves in the process.

What does it take to make a successful business organization? The same thing it takes to make a championship sports team or to put someone on the moon—a group of creative individuals having fun *doing their thing* together. Such groups have strong leaders; they joke often and kid each other regularly. They frequently express mutual caring and respect, and they laugh a lot. Why not picture yourself not so much as a boss but as a conductor, leading instead of commanding?

You may be a bit skeptical about this idea. How can having fun be all that crucial if so many workplaces still haven't made it a priority? John Sculley, CEO of Apple Computer, notes in his book Odyssey: Pepsi to Apple ... A Journey of Adventure, Ideas, and the Future, "Virtually all our models of motivation derive from industrial or post-industrial labor." Some businesses either aren't aware or don't care that what worked back then no longer applies in today's age of high technology or to a generation of workers who consciously or subconsciously demand job satisfaction.

It is an unhappy fact that too many companies still have little regard for individuals. Workers are demeaned, and spirits are diminished. The result is unreached potential, for both the workers and the company. Often those who complain and quit are rebelling in the only way they know against a system they feel powerless to change.

In his best-selling *Reinventing the Corporation*, author John Naisbitt gives a good insight into the evolution of the workplace. In the beginning it flourished through money and machines, but most businesses today find that their chief assets are information, knowledge, and creativity. Emphasis has shifted from financial resources to human resources. Since using resources profitably is what management is all about, effective managers must search for and adopt whatever methods produce the best results. Looking at today's successful workplaces, you will see they have in common teamwork, mutual caring and respect, laughter, and a zest for achieving.

To fully appreciate the role humor and fun can play in increasing production, consider the changes that have taken place over the past fifty years. People fifty years old or older have seen the introduction of most of the significant inventions benefiting the masses. They preceded television, air conditioners, clothes dryers, electric typewriters, credit cards, ballpoint pens, and yogurt In fact, more has happened within the past 45 years than in the previous 4,500 years; more than 85 percent of all great scientists who ever lived are living today. Furthermore, those born before 1940 can remember a time when closets were for clothes rather than for *coming out of*; when "setting the world on fire" was merely a figure of speech; when health foods were what your mother said you had better eat or else; when the question "Is it a boy or a girl?" referred only to newborn babies; when clothes had labels on the inside.

Very few people living during the Industrial Revolution had any appreciation of what was happening. Generally they were unaware of living through what was, up until that time, the greatest era of significant change ever to take place. But in today's Information Age, workers are aware of the important roles they play. Thus this latter revolution has had substantial impact on nearly all aspects of our lives and has changed the workplace tremendously.

John Naisbitt points out in Megatrends that more than half of all income in this country now comes from services instead of manufactured goods. In the evolving service economy, astute companies and their managers are placing more emphasis on their people.

To avoid losing their more creative and enterprising people, many companies are now giving these types funding, time, and most importantly encouragement to dream up new products. So-called "intrapreneurial teams" are responsible for the development of Apple's Macintosh, IBM's personal computer, and 3M's very popular Post-It Notes. These teams, rather than the traditional research and development departments, are not only coming up with innovative and profitable new products but are developing cost-saving measures as well. The atmosphere of the workplace is crucial in setting the stage for this kind of initiative.

A good-humored, creative environment is every bit as important to factories as it is to think tanks. Fun may have to take a different form in less creative surroundings, but it shouldn't be dismissed as *inappropriate*.

A good sense of humor is equally crucial to an entrepreneur or small business owner. When asked what his sense of humor had done for his career, Renn Zaphiropoulos, cofounder and president of Versatec in Silicon Valley, said, "It has given me the courage to go through rough times." And as any entrepreneur will gladly tell you, there will be rough times. Paul Hawkins, entrepreneur and host of the TV series "Growing a Business," contends, "If you and your employees, customers, and vendors don't have a good time, if the laughter has died, you're in the wrong business." In fact, virtually all the experts say that, if you want a small business to succeed, you have to make it fun.

Every business person needs the extra edge that humor gives. Whether you are enjoying the power of an established CEO, assuming your first managerial position, changing workplaces, or moving up, your sense of humor will be one of your most valuable assets. The more differences there are between you and your workmates—in ethnic background, gender, age, culture, education, religion—the more necessary your sense of humor is. Your ability to put things into proper perspective and laugh will carry you through the initial stages of your career and through any challenges that might arise.

Two

Behavioral Modes

You can't shake hands with a clenched fist.
—Golda Meir

Did you know that everyone you deal with is functioning in one or the other of two modes? The modes are open and closed.

In the closed mode, we are guarded and reserved; we don't want to appear silly or stupid. In this mode we are very protective of the status quo, tending to dislike change and to be unreceptive to new ideas. We generally look closed, with our arms and perhaps our legs crossed. In the closed mode we are given to formality, structure, and at times pomposity.

In the industrial era, money and machines were chief resources; workers were secondary. In large part, companies were buying workers' motions. Making assembly-line, mass-production jobs fun would have been difficult and might have detracted from the function of the workplace. From the standpoint of the employer, the closed mode was most profitable. Employee participation in management was neither actively sought nor welcomed.

The closed mode is still encouraged in some companies. Ask just about any dissatisfied worker.

The open mode is quite different. We become relaxed, lighten up, and share verbally. We give ourselves and those around us permission to be frivolous. We are not overly concerned about saying something silly or off the mark. This open mode goes hand in hand with informality and spontaneity. It gives us the insight to be highly receptive to new ideas and the willingness to give change a chance. This mode is reflected in our body language: arms rest comfortably, hands unclench, and legs relax.

It is in this mode and this mode alone that we are truly creative. When the conscious mind relaxes, the subconscious mind, the seat of all creativity, is free to function. Activities like jogging, playing golf, bicycling, and looking out a window, which lull the conscious mind, sometimes bring forth the best ideas. Similarly, during sleep the conscious mind goes into a state of deep relaxation, and the subconscious effortlessly produces the mental theater we call dreams. Many who have found this to be true keep a pad and pen or a tape recorder beside the bed so as not to lose the creative thoughts that linger when awakening from a dream.

The first step in learning how to use humor as a tool for communicating is to learn how to recognize the mode of your audience, whether it is one person or a roomful of people. The moods and behavior confronting you can usually, if not always, be associated with one of the two modes. The open mode is democratic, exploratory, playful, candid, and conducive to risk taking; the closed mode fosters a tighter, more rigid, conservative, hierarchical, solemn, narrow-visioned approach.

The open mode is not appropriate in every instance; each mode has its proper time and place. When the ship is sinking, a responsible leader does not call for participative decision making. Someone must give unchallenged orders and be followed without question. But if participation, receptivity, and creativity are desirable, everyone involved must be in an open mode. Sometimes both modes come into play—for example, during a football game. When the team is in a huddle, the quarterback usually accepts others' ideas and observations. Once the play is called, however, the other players follow the plan without hesitation and in accordance with the playbook.

Three

What Motivates Employees

Money will buy a pretty good dog, but it won't buy the wag of his tail.
—Josh Billings

In the past, job security and money were the top motivators. Today, with mergers, buyouts, and international competition, there is no such thing as real job security. The only real job security any of us has is our own package of marketable skills. What's more, most surveys on job satisfaction show that money is no longer even one of the top three motivators. Job challenges, respect, and a sense of accomplishment are more energizing than a fat paycheck. What employees may miss in hard currency can be more than compensated for in the soft currencies of human resource management.

Thus today's manager must have strong motivational and people skills. When seeking worker input, the most effective thing an astute manager can do is to create among the employees a sense of camaraderie and fun. Fun is not simply a perk; it is a way of increasing production and energizing the workforce. It is, in short, motivating.

People are easiest to motivate when they are in the open mode. Humor is one of the quickest ways to foster an open mode, but you can't keep employees supplied with humor on a full-time basis. However, fun and play can be present much of the time. Hiring people who are predisposed to having a good time while doing their jobs is also helpful. They bring a lot of self-motivation to the job with them.

The idea is to make work environments pleasurable, generating self-fulfilling positive attitudes. If you think your work is too mundane for this, take another look at what your *real job* is. Reconsider your mission. Employees at Apple Computer, for example, don't see themselves as *making computers* but rather as *changing peoples' lives*. Sometimes we have to look beyond the task to find the mission.

Not long ago, a motivational consultant visited an aerospace company in Southern California. The company's senior vice president confessed his puzzlement at the remarkable attitudes of the employees who maintained the pipes in the thermodynamics plant. Their job was to check temperatures and pressures of pipes that had to work within strict tolerances; any malfunction would produce expensive damage to delicate equipment. In spite of the work being repetitive and mechanical, the employees' attendance record was exceptional, their turnover rate the lowest in the company, their productivity and performance excellent, and their motivation obviously high. The vice president wondered how they delivered peak performances consistently.

The consultant visited the department and was shown around by the foreman. The workers all wore green surgical gowns, which the foreman had obtained from his son, a cardiovascular surgeon. The consultant said, "Ah, so you wear them for comfort?" "No, no," answered the foreman, "it's because we are surgeons. Just like my son. He takes care of pipes of the body—we take care of pipes of the plant. The plant isn't going to have any breakdowns as long as we're working on its arteries. We take care of these pipes the way a doctor takes care of your heart." The analogy extended even to workers' locker doors, which were stenciled with their names, preceded by "Dr."

The point is that these workers had a sense of mission translated into a fun thing. It gave their work special value and kept them performing at peak level. If the work in your workplace is repetitive and mechanical, you might consider a similar method of motivating your team.

Yes, you can buy a very good dog. A top CEO noted, following his retirement, "You can hire the best employee. You can spend lots of money and furnish him with the very best training. You can even purchase a predetermined number of specific mechanical movements. But you can't buy his commitment—you have to earn that!"

Four

What Humor Is

*Humor provides us with a valuable tool for maintaining
an inner strength in the midst of outer turmoil.*
—Brian Deery

The relationship between employer and employee is inherently strained. The employee's financial dependence on the employer is naturally intimidating, and the two often have different financial, cultural, and educational backgrounds. Management's and labor's interests in the business aren't the same, and they are compensated at different levels and for different reasons.

The manager who wants cooperation from an employee must begin by removing or reducing the intimidation. This is where humor can play a crucial role. It has the power to bridge gaps and, when desirable, to serve as a leveler. Thus it has an important role from the very first meeting. If you do not establish an atmosphere that lets the prospective employee open up, you won't really see the person you're hiring. You may pay for the oversight for a long time.

There are only three ways to get anyone to do anything: threaten, bribe, or cajole. Humor, which is subtle cajoling, creates a common ground and fosters the desire to achieve mutual goals. Without humor, you will find yourself trying to attain your goals through one of the less attractive alternatives.

Humor comes in diverse forms, jokes, quips, games, puns, and anecdotes being only a few. And good humor does not have to be verbal. In fact, it is often an aura.

There is frivolous humor and nonfrivolous humor. For anyone who frowns on frivolity, it is important to note that being humorous doesn't have to mean being frivolous. Not that frivolity is bad; it is just not always desirable. There are times when frivolity and creative silliness will produce a mind-set desirable for a certain purpose. With guidance, the ensuing good humor will not invite inappropriate actions or diminish the serious nature of the matter at hand.

Although humor can be present during serious times, it is not compatible with solemnity. John Cleese, actor, writer, director, and founder of Video Arts, a company that produces training films, makes one of the best arguments against solemnity of any I have read. In an article in Manager's Journal titled "Serious Talk About Humor in the Office," he says, "The value of solemnity is overrated because it often induces in people feelings of pomposity, rigidity, and a corresponding loss of ordinary human warmth and easy, open communications." You can simultaneously be humorous and very serious, but you cannot maintain solemnity and still foster humor.

But who needs to be solemn to be productive? This misconception is probably responsible for the absence of humor in too many board rooms and executive suites. Even those who would like to introduce humor may fear that doing so will diminish the importance of their mission or signal their subordinates that they lack seriousness of purpose. Quite the contrary! A sense of humor sends messages of self-confidence, security, and control over the situation. It is when control is missing that humor turns into *goofing off*. Properly instituted and directed, humor will set the guidelines for those who don't recognize the difference.

So what is a sense of humor? What is your definition? Some say it is the ability to recognize and express merriment. For me, it is thinking funny and being able to laugh at one's self.

The importance of learning how to laugh at yourself cannot be overstated. First of all, in practical terms, laughing at yourself (self-directed humor) is often the only kind that will accomplish your purpose. Second, the capacity for seeing humor in your own actions is a sign of maturity and self-confidence. Laughing with others about your own foibles is a way of showing that you recognize your shortcomings but still feel you are okay.

A sense of humor has become an integral part of the personality of every modern leader. It is part of *charisma*, a subject that will come up again later in the book. Just look at official photographs of U.S. Presidents and other leaders over the years. At the turn of the century, they all looked stern and solemn. Today's leaders, often casually posed, relaxed, and smiling, project a more favorable image. Humor, once an admirable character trait, has become mandatory.

> *Humor is not spiteful, but rather it is sympathetic*
> *to the difficulties of human survival.*

Some people think they are *funny* but are decidedly not. Memories of such a person may keep you from using humor, fun, and enjoyment in every facet of your life. But if you follow the general guidelines in this book, you won't have to worry about hurting anyone with your well-developed sense of humor.

Sarcastic or scornful humor may make people laugh, but it won't build trust or respect or influence them in a positive way. If humor causes embarrassment or hurt feelings, if it makes something that someone values look common, or if it *blows out another's candle to make yours appear brighter*, it isn't humor. Too many comedians use inappropriate material to get a quick (albeit uneasy) laugh, and they give humor a bad name. Good humor does not destroy confidence or teamwork, nor does it single out individuals or groups to inflict pain upon.

It is important to emphasize, and difficult to overstate, the point: Fun and enjoyment belong in the workplace. Humor is simply the easiest and most certain way to assure fun. Fun is not necessarily humor, but humor is by definition fun. One of the reasons for emphasizing this point is to reassure you. You do not need to become a comedian; you are not aiming for a continuous stream of leg slappers. You just want to provide amusement, some smiles and occasional laughter. If you find that your efforts are producing a lot of big laughs, you may want to consider quitting your job and going on stage for the really big bucks. But if your success is more modest, you can take advantage of the productive and enjoyable working environment you're creating.

Five

Company Policies

To err is human; to forgive is against company policy.

Does your workplace reflect out-of-date dictates or newer, more desirable ones? In the past, managers expounded on "not letting the inmates run the asylum." Workers responded by mouthing "Thank God, it's almost quitting time" or the popular T.G.I.F. ("Thank God, it's Friday"). Their formula was "Let's put in our hours and get it over with; in the meantime, let's try to get along as best we can." Employees did indeed have the attitude that work was their punishment for not marrying rich!

Today it is not unusual to find workplaces with opposite attitudes. Not long ago, I was treated to an environment, a video production company, in which the workers were encouraged to create and to enjoy themselves. Good humor was reflected everywhere, especially in the amount and quality of the work being done. I listened as one employee spoke enthusiastically of coming in over the weekend to work on a project. Employees took just enough time for lunch to grab a sandwich in the small kitchen on the premises. Although I spent an entire day there producing a video and interacted with all of the staff, I couldn't tell who was in charge of whom. The place was replete with humor and friendly kidding. Clearly these people enjoyed their work and looked forward to coming to the workplace.

Before you write off your company as totally unreceptive to good humor and participation, remember that organizations are changed from within by individuals. Perhaps you can start the ball rolling in your workplace by heeding the advice of former President Gerald Ford. At the close of a seminar, he stated,"It would be a good idea for people in business and other professions—especially ones that have an exaggerated opinion of their power and influence—to be able to laugh at themselves."

Good public and internal relations are created by establishing an informal, creative atmosphere where ideas and opinions can be exchanged. I can think of no better way of opening the lines of communication than with a good-humored approach. Today's leaders are reaping the benefits from this concept.

When Lee Iacocca became CEO of Chrysler Motors, the company looked like a lost cause. Much has been written about his belief in getting the cooperation and participation of his employees. According to sources, one of his first acts was to meet with his plant managers on their turf and ask for their input. Reportedly he took off his suit coat, loosened his tie, and rolled up his sleeves before going into the factory. During the meeting, he had lemonade and cookies served to his front-line managers. In this good-humored, informal setting, he asked them what they thought he ought to do. It is said this was not a one-time thing—he continued looking to them for their input. Iacocca credited his front-line managers for 80 percent of the ideas used to turn Chrysler Motors around.

I wonder how many of those ideas would have been offered if Iacocca had called those same people into his board room and sat solemnly at the head of a highly polished table. Effective executives who successfully draw on the resources of their people know the formula: Informality and spontaneity foster open communications and stimulate creativity. The key is to remove the intimidation inherent in employer-employee relationships. There's no quicker way to accomplish this than through your sense of humor.

Even industries with the heaviest, most serious responsibilities—such as banking, education, medicine, and public service—don't have to be humorless. Actually, men and women in these occupations are often in the greatest need of drama-relieving humor.

Banking

Traditionally, banks have had an image of being stodgy, dreary institutions. After all, it would hardly be proper for those who handle depositors' hard-earned cash, and who are regulated by the comptrollers of the national currency, to engage in fits of giggles. Even I might be put off if I saw people responsible for my money engaging in spitball battles.

It used to be said that the ideal banker was bald, with a substantial paunch and a good case of hemorrhoids. The baldness denoted maturity and the paunch prosperity, and the hemorrhoids were supposed to provide a look of concern. Today's leaders in financial fields in no way fit that description, nor do they need to.

The relationships among banks, their customers, and their employees are changing. In practically all cases, good humor and fun are a part of these new attitudes. One bank sponsors a family night each quarter. Families and guests of employees are invited to watch the routine followed to close the bank. The bank then treats everybody to dinner. These events boost employee morale and help employees' families understand why they sometimes have to work late.

Bank of America reportedly sponsors joke-telling contests among its employees. Arizona BancWest Corp. ran a $3.5 million humorous ad campaign in 1982. It was highly successful, resulting in 97 percent name recognition among Arizona consumers and double the previous growth in new accounts. And a bank in Palo Alto, California decorated the side of its building with an alien getting out of a flying saucer that had crashed into the bank. Evidently, management of that bank enjoys laughing and wants its public to laugh also.

Education

It seems nowadays that an eager, happy group of students is a media event. Ken Blanchard, author of *The One-Minute Manager*, has consulted with a number of school districts. He noted in an interview in *Laughing Matters* that "nobody in school was having fun anymore. The kids didn't want to be there; the teachers didn't want to be there; the principal didn't want to be there; even the janitors who used to do most of the counseling down in the boiler room didn't want to be there. Laughter is a lost art. Nothing in schools can be that serious, I mean, we're dealing with kids' lives—we need to laugh."

I recently read that children normally laugh an average of 500 times a day, adults 15 times. If children aren't getting their daily dose of laughter and aren't being taught the value of good humor during their formative years, what kind of adults will they become? A close examination of our culture will reveal various ways we discourage young people from laughing openly and easily. We teach them to be overly serious and solemn. This is a mistake at a time when we need a good sense of humor and a lot of laughter just to maintain our good health. Fortunately, we can teach ourselves to laugh more and to see the humorous side of things.

Jim Vlassis, principal of Mira Mesa High School in San Diego, has found that he can get away with hanging a spoon from his nose at boring meetings, and he does so at many functions, no matter how formal. He says that part of his philosophy is to have fun and that no one has more fun working than he does. Since Mr. Vlassis became the high school's principal, truancy rates have dropped, test scores have improved, and he has been heralded as an effective educator.

A friend of mine taught a structured reading course to groups of disadvantaged children. She had a good sense of humor, which she relayed to the students and used herself to keep from becoming discouraged. Not only did she help the children improve their reading skills, but when they returned to their classrooms, their regular teachers noted a remarkable difference in their ability to join in and comprehend in other areas.

Another teacher started the day off with a smile by writing on her attendance report, "Help! They're all here today!" She cheered up herself and the office staff.

Teachers often meet in the lounge and put themselves in a negative mood by complaining about everything. A friend who taught said she was so depressed each morning after leaving the lounge that facing her first-period class became an overwhelming chore. She arrived late one day, missed coffee in the lounge, and found herself teaching with renewed zeal. She began staying away from the lounge but found she missed her peers. What was lacking in the teachers' lounge, she decided, was good humor. Now she and her fellow teachers use their time in the lounge to share cartoons, jokes, comedy tapes—and most important, instead of telling student horror tales, they tell student success stories. This is something you might try if your school is lacking in good humor, fun, and enjoyment.

Health Care

I will admit sincerely hoping, for my own sake, that members of the medical profession take their jobs seriously. But is any workplace in greater need of good humor and fun? Studies show that humor eases pain and heals. They show also that incompetent doctors with a good bedside manner are less likely to be sued than doctors with a poor bedside manner.

In a recent flu epidemic, I felt I had been attacked more viciously than anyone else in the country. I was sick and depressed. Feeling guilty and defensive, I finally gave in and made an appointment to visit a doctor. He subtly reassured me with his good-humored attitude. After taking one look at me, he smiled and said, "A thing like this sure humbles a person, doesn't it?" By the time I left his office, and before I'd even gotten a prescription filled, his good *bedside manner* had already made me feel better.

An aide in one hospital makes the trip for tests more bearable by kidding the patient who is being pushed in a wheelchair, "Sit back and relax—and you can stop looking down at the floor. There's no money there, and if there was, I could beat you to it anyway!"

Public Service

Many public-service occupations create excessive job-related stress, such as social work, law enforcement, fire fighting, and combat. Workers who are risking their lives or relating to people in intolerable situations over which they have little control sometimes keep sane by resorting to grotesque humor. Called *gallow's*, *black*, *graveyard*, even *sick* humor, it ranges from absurd to revolting. It usually comes out of frustration, anger, or pain.

Probably one of the best-known examples of this kind of humor is the "M.A.S.H." television series, which is about medical personnel in a war setting. Practically everyone has been exposed to Hawkeye's and B.J.'s unorthodox ways of coping with tragedy.

Welfare workers often squeeze humor out of their correspondence: "I am forwarding my marriage certificate and six children, I had seven but one died which was baptized on a half sheet of paper." Or "Mrs. Jones hasn't had any clothes for a year and has been visited regularly by the clergy." Or "My husband got his project cut off two weeks ago and I haven't had any relief since."

Joseph Wambaugh, in *The Choirboys*, gives a rather graphic example of the kind of humor that sometimes erupts in stressful situations. He writes that the police are annoyed at accident scenes by *rubber-necks*, who drive by very slowly so they can gawk at the crash site. In one particular accident, a woman was decapitated. The police encountered the usual line of cars bearing curious onlookers. An automobile with license plates from the Midwest pulled up, and the driver asked the usual question: "Was anybody hurt?" One of the police officers lifted the severed head of the victim by the hair and said, "Well, this one was banged up a little bit!"

People who deal with these kinds of situations know that sometimes they have to start laughing so they don't start crying. The fact that gallows humor is so common during extremely emotional times indicates that humor is a natural stress-release mechanism for human beings. A response that would be inappropriate at any other time or in any other place puts us in a frame of mind to carry on and do what must be done.

Six

Management Styles

When management wants your opinion, they'll give it to you!

Companies usually let managers know, by example or rules, what management style they prefer. Among those styles are the authoritative style, in which no employee input is asked for or appreciated; the traditional style, which is less dictatorial than the authoritarian style but does emphasize control; the consultative style, in which the manager consults with employees but makes the decision alone and issues directions for implementing change; and the participative style, in which the manager determines policy or procedure with the participation of employees.

The consultative and participative styles of management are becoming more prevalent, but some successful companies still cling to the old ways. It is my opinion that they may be successful in the short term but will not benefit all they can until they tap the knowledge of the employees they have hired. They will end up spending too much time maintaining the status quo instead of rushing ahead.

There's another way to look at management style: You can manage activity, or you can manage results. A friend of mine was involved in an activity-managed job while working at a shipyard in Virginia. He was there as a *governmental requirement* and had very little to do. Occasionally he would stay late and use the copy machine to reproduce the text of a novel.

During the next workday, he would be seen carefully studying a tall stack of *work papers*. In actuality, he was enjoying a well-written mystery, but he gave the impression of being a hard-working guy who was going places in that company.

The movie *How To Succeed in Business Without Really Trying* also showed how easily the illusion of *busy-ness* can be accomplished. After everyone else left the office, the young advertising executive gathered all the ashtrays and dumped them into his own to make it look as though he had worked late into the evening.

If we could properly channel workers' creativity and the energy they use to appear busy, imagine how much could be accomplished. One adage states, "Millions of Americans aren't working—but thank God they've got jobs!" And in the 1970s, people who were employed by *activity managers* used the term "shucking and jiving," which meant going through the motions to make your supervisor believe you were hard at work. It was basically an acting job.

Management Versus Leadership

You probably are familiar with the axiom that most of today's companies are *overmanaged and underled*. What is the difference between leadership and management? The usual distinction is that management is driving, reliant on authority, and based on fear, whereas leadership is coaching, reliant on goodwill, and based on enthusiasm and inspiration. Management authority is bestowed, deriving from the top down. Leadership is earned, and it emanates from the bottom up. The modern, progressive manager is seen as more of a coach than a commander, more as a rudder than a propeller.

President Dwight Eisenhower demonstrated his theory of leadership with a piece of string. Placing it on the table, he would push one end of the string toward the other. "See, when I push it, it doesn't go anywhere!" he would say. Then he would take the other end and gently pull it. "Look," he would say, "if I pull it, I can take it anywhere I want." Leaders are followed!

Authority and leadership are not the same thing. Authority is vested in a manager by virtue of tangible power; leadership is acquired through one's personal skills.

Effective leadership influences people pleasantly. Influential leaders initiate the goodwill inherent in a humor- and fun-filled environment.

Authoritative and Traditional Management

For the last two hundred years, we've been using the Catholic Church and Caesar's legions as patterns for creating organizations. —Robert Townsend

The model of management presented by the church and the military relies on secrecy at the top, orders handed down and followed without question, a clear chain of command, and strong leadership. Managers who use this authoritative style expect—nay, demand—conformity. Dress codes, even when unnecessary, are strictly enforced. Blue shirts, red ties, clean-shaven faces, and other such things are sometimes the order of the day. Personal input or individualism is neither invited nor acceptable.

Organizations like these often take their management team off to retreats where they dress very casually and brainstorm in a relaxed atmosphere. You would think they would recognize that creativity flourishes in the open mode and then try it in the workplace. Yet the moment they return, they fall immediately into the mold of conformity, leaving behind any progress they could have instituted. Workers joke that managers go away to retreats to relieve their own stress while creating ways to make workers' lives more stressful.

The drill sergeant management style is rapidly going out of style, even in the military. It is demeaning, creates resentment, and is responsible for low morale and increased dissatisfaction and absenteeism. Today's employee is simply too well educated and financially independent and has too many options for this to work.

How well today's employees would accept Henry Ford's dictatorial manner is questionable. When one of Ford's managers debated a point with him, he would say, "Let's go outside and see whose name is on the building." Wouldn't you just bet that his attitude was reflected down the line?

Tyrannical managerial behavior leaves employees confused. Imagine working for movie mogul Samuel Goldwyn, who reportedly said, "I don't want any yes-men around me. I want everybody to tell me the truth, even if it costs them their jobs." Is there any question that suppressing employee opinion is counterproductive? How can it possibly foster goodwill toward the organization and a positive attitude about the workplace?

Many modern companies still operate in this fashion, but many others are looking for a better way. Leaders are realizing that they must come to grips with open discussion, conflict, and resolution. They work—trying to control the employee does not! Today's workers measure satisfaction less in terms of money than in terms of personal fulfillment. Humor is invaluable for initiating the necessary openness and retaining it.

Consultative and Participative Management

The more a company wants the participation, commitment, and creativity of its employees, the more important it is to establish a comfortable, relaxed, and open work environment. The need for employee cooperation has made the consultative and participative styles of management more popular. Humor goes hand in hand with management that encourages individuals to enjoy the 39 percent of their lives they spend in the workplace.

The consultative and participative management styles are enhanced by a sort of contrarianism, which assumes that, if two people have exactly the same ideas and agree on everything, then the company can get along with only one of them. Alfred Sloan, legendary president of General Motors in the 1920s, was said to value this kind of thinking. At a meeting of his top managers, when everyone voiced support for one of his proposals, he moved to postpone further discussion on the matter until the next morning, "to give ourselves time to develop disagreement and perhaps gain some understanding of what this decision is about."

Some contemporary managers use the Socratic method for gaining diverse opinions. One of these is August Busch III, CEO of Anheuser-Busch. When tough issues are on the agenda, he sets up a forum where two executives take opposing points of view.

Contrarian thinking exists in most organizations, but it is rarely expressed. If you believe that examining issues from different perspectives leads to quality decisions, you must take special care to convey this belief through your behavior. Employees won't participate without your encouragement. They've learned that many organizations *shoot the messenger* who brings unwelcome news or other information they don't particularly want to hear. If you really want to reap the benefits of contrarian thinking, you must let employees know that they are welcome to speak out, that contrarian views are actually appreciated and valued.

A manager's use of humor is the most effective signal that he or she approves of openness. Remember that participative communication relies on informality, relaxation, spontaneity, fun, openness, humor, and nonstandard thinking, all of which are manifestations of the open mode.

Seven

Humor: A Multipurpose Marvel

Human beings are the only animals that laugh, because only human beings know what ought to be. Laughter between people is subtle acknowledgment that we are all brothers and sisters —all in this thing called "life" together.

Take a moment and recall how many situations in the past twenty-four hours have been dealt with positively by someone with a good sense of humor. What did the humor accomplish? It may have been used to maintain control, build morale and teamwork, relieve tension, chide, overcome a difficult situation, make a point, sell a product, defuse criticism.

Humor is not only versatile, it is also insidious. You may plan to use it to accomplish only one goal, but you will soon see it spread and rebound. What builds rapport often defuses criticism, relieves tension, and creates numerous other trickle-down benefits. I cannot think of anything else that is so useful. Humor is indeed a multipurpose marvel.

Humor Signifies Control

A speaker I know was attempting to get started with his presentation but was encountering an array of difficulties. First he dropped his notes on the floor. Then the microphone he had attached to his lapel fell off and landed on the floor with a loud thud. When it looked as though he had everything under control, the microphone began emitting loud screeches. He stopped, looked out at the audience, and asked, "How do you like it so far?" This little comment broke up the crowd. The audience, reassured that he was in control, prepared to listen to what he had to say. That one short quip turned him from a loser into a winner.

Sometimes you can prepare ahead for situations in which you must either regain control or concede defeat. More often, unexpected events require you to *think on your feet*. As you develop the style of humor that fits your personality, spontaneous humor will come easier. In either case, quips that turn attention back where it belongs usually are your best bet.

I like the way a woman speaking at a large banquet regained control when a busboy began clearing a table in front of the podium. Pausing a second, she gestured smilingly toward the young man and said, "Of course, all of you know my husband." With this remark she directed the crowd's attention away from the distraction and back to her.

I once attended a meeting where a highly placed state official was giving a somewhat bureaucratic presentation to a large group. In the middle of his talk, someone began pounding on one of the auditorium doors. Without missing a beat, the speaker, obviously adept at handling impromptu situations, said, "Now there's a switch—someone trying to get in!"

Humor Builds Teams and Boosts Morale

> *It's easy to get good players. Gettin' 'em to*
> *play together, that's the hard part.*   —Casey Stengel

There is no question that organizations where people like and are loyal to one another experience better cooperation and accomplish more. Teamwork is the foundation of effective performance.

If you study winning teams, you'll find strong leaders—as well as good humor, camaraderie, fun, and a sense of mission. A sense of mission goes hand in hand with a sense of humor. They complement each other and set up the potential for self-fulfillment. Picture in your mind some finely tuned teams with high morale, enthusiasm, the ability to think creatively and to cooperate within the group. Now picture any of these teams trying to function in an atmosphere of formality and pomposity. I'll bet that you can see the incongruity.

An earlier statement is worth repeating: Winning teams joke a lot, kid one another regularly, and laugh together a great deal. This is no accident. These are signs of caring and sharing. The humor sets up a framework for drawing on every team member's strengths, which creates a synergistic effort.

Some managers are disturbed by the sound of laughter. But they should rethink their concerns, because a number of studies have shown that laughter could be a sign of rising production. The lesson is to create opportunities for the regular use of fun at your workplace.

During war time, pilots painted smiles on their planes and gave them names that amused their buddies. Two rather successful men who named their planes after the girls they loved were President George Bush and General Charles Yaeger. Both are noted for inspiring team efforts and boosting morale.

When sports teams are at their winningest, dozens of stories are told of their inside jokes and their fun together. A team might be exhorted to "win one for the Gipper"; they might do *shuffles*, *flips*, or *high fives* to celebrate a score; they might come up with nicknames denoting affection, such as *The Three Amigos* or *The Hawgs*. Camaraderie can be displayed any number of ways, but they all celebrate the teamwork that makes them winners.

Humor Relieves Tension

Humor can be an effective—and indispensable—tool in dealing with tension and hostility. When we laugh or even smile, we relax. Correctly executed, humor does not detract from the serious nature of the problem, but it does open the mind to creative solutions.

One of the most tense situations affecting the entire world was the Cuban missile crisis in the 1960s. The U.S. government had ordered the Soviet Union to remove its missiles from Cuba, or else! Meanwhile, a group of distinguished Soviet and American citizens happened to be meeting to promote international understanding. As you can imagine, things got more than a little tense. One of the Americans suggested that they drop discussion of the missile crisis and each tell their favorite story. A Russian was the first to speak up: "What is the difference between capitalism and communism?" With perfect timing, he answered, "In capitalism, man exploits man; in communism, it's the other way around." Meeting participants eventually returned to the business at hand with a new vision of their mutual concerns.

Several years ago, Eugene Cafiero, president of Chrysler Motors, went to England to meet with workers at a troubled plant. As he was ushered in to meet with union bosses, he was confronted by a man who loudly proclaimed, "I'm Eddie McCluskey, and I'm a Communist!" Cafiero, extended his hand and said, "How do you do? I'm Eugene Cafiero, and I'm a Presbyterian." This is an excellent example of the use of humor to break tension, defuse hostility, and still maintain control of the situation.

During the early 1970s, I was involved in urban revitalization and therefore present at many community meetings roiling with controversy. At one, a heated debate about a policy of the federal government was becoming even hotter. One of the debaters related that he had written to the President, protesting the policy and explaining why it was ill advised. The other debater rose to defend the controversial policy and said it surely would endure, because the President recently had endorsed it publicly. As he sat down, his opponent stood and exclaimed, "That was before he got my letter!" The laughter that followed eased the tension and provided a badly needed respite.

Since one of the manager's duties is to resolve personality conflicts that hamper productivity, becoming adept at using humor to relieve tension is a worthwhile goal. Remember that the key to defusing tension with humor is to use the self-directed kind, at least in the beginning. Always laugh at yourself first. That is a way of saying "I can laugh at myself; I don't take myself too seriously; I am confident and secure, are you?" If you've just made fun of yourself, others will have trouble taking umbrage at some good-natured humor directed at them. Personality conflicts are usually based on rather minor items and can easily be handled by showing the participants how trivial their differences are. Humor is an excellent way to display that fact.

Humor Chides

Offering a reproval wrapped as good-natured chiding often will get the message across so you don't have to resort to harsher measures. I discovered quite a while ago that my anger can call up a whole armory of defensive weapons and give others an opening to blast away. Neither person benefits, and nothing is settled. A genuine smile and a "looks like you and I are having a bad day" acknowledges that there is a problem but indicates that you prefer not to handle it negatively. You are sending a message that you are not blaming the other person for the situation but are not acknowledging fault either. In turn, the other party will feel secure enough to acknowledge culpability.

A California bank, when contacting customers with longstanding overdrafts, wrote, "Dear Customer: We would be most grateful if we could revert to the old system of you banking with us."

"I'm collecting," said the paper boy. "Very good," said the customer with a wide grin, "Your money is over there in the bushes where I usually find my paper."

After several unsuccessful attempts to get across the message to a secretary who, except for her typing, had wonderful skills, the manager got a schedule from a community college, circled the Typing 101 course, and noted with a smile that there was an opening in the next class.

When Grace's pay envelope came to her desk empty, she called accounting and asked good-naturedly if her deductions had finally caught up with her salary. She was tempted to air every complaint she'd ever had against that department. Instead, her humorous approach kept the lines of communication open and enabled both parties to solve the problem without losing face.

Some politicians are masters of this chiding humor. I know a politician back in Ohio who used humor in answering letters that questioned his intelligence and sometimes his parentage. He'd send the letter back to its author with a note: "The enclosed letter arrived on my desk a few days ago. I'm sending it to you in the belief that, as a responsible citizen, you should know that some crank is sending out this kind of drivel in letters over your signature."

Humor Gives Perspective and Solves Problems

There are three things which are real: God,
human folly, and laughter. The first two are
beyond our comprehension. So we must do what
we can with the third.   —John F. Kennedy

A large part of any problem is the seriousness with which we view it. In problem solving, perspective is everything. Beginning to solve a difficult problem by stepping back and viewing its parts in proper perspective is absolutely invaluable. By the way, perspective is the ability to view distance as well as foreground.

The next step in problem solving is to activate your creativity. You can get the creative juices flowing by relaxing your conscious mind and freeing up your subconscious, which is the seat of all creativity. Structure and formality inhibit communications and stifle creativity. What setting is more informal and spontaneous—and therefore more likely to foster creative problem solving—than one with good humor, fun, and play?

I gather from everything I've read or heard about Walt Disney that he was a genius at solving problems creatively. As opening day at Disneyland rapidly approached, funds were running low and the landscaping was not finished. Disney came up with a solution that only someone with perspective could have. Since all the other plants were labeled with their Latin names, he told the gardener to find the Latin names for the weeds in the park and label them too. He really knew how to take a lemon and make lemonade! Perhaps it is noteworthy that Michael Eisner, the current CEO of Disney Productions, is an advocate of fun on the job, believing it to be one of the ingredients of successful management. He is also one of the most highly touted and lavishly paid CEOs on the scene today.

Of course, people in the business of entertaining have solved problems creatively as long as show business has existed. P. T. Barnum, the circus impresario, died a hundred years ago but is still remembered for his style and flair. When congestion in the aisles of Barnum's side show became a problem, he kept the crowds moving with a sign that read "This Way to the Egress." Not until they found the *egress* did they realize they'd been led to the exit.

In addition to fostering creativity, humor gives perspective. It provides balanced observation and draws people into an open mode.

A fourteen-year-old girl came home from school and announced to her family that she was pregnant. After all the commotion died down, she said, "I'm not really pregnant, but I did flunk history, and I wanted to put things into perspective."

Many knowledgeable people and organizations use humor to provide perspective. For example, *Newsweek* magazine puts a page of humorous quotes and quips near the front of each issue, to give perspective to the weightier matter in the rest of the magazine.

Humor not only enables us to put things into perspective for others; more importantly, it can help us see ourselves in a more realistic light. Stepping back and viewing a problem with a certain level of detachment restores perspective. This is the reasoning behind the legal axiom that a lawyer who defends himself has a fool for a client. Sometimes, if you exaggerate a problem, you can then laugh at it or at least decrease its intensity: "Is it going to kill me? Will it start a war? Will it matter a year from now?" How many times have you said to yourself, "A year from now, I'll laugh at this!" But why wait a year; why not laugh now?

Humor Makes Unavoidable Circumstances Tolerable

Perhaps you've heard of ministers who, in conducting funeral services, always try to include the deceased's favorite joke in the eulogy. They find that the joke provides a temporary respite from grief and brings back warm memories of happier times. This is an observation, not advice for handling individual situations during periods of mourning. When people who have experienced a death start laughing again, you'll know the healing process has begun.

In the business world, a plush, hushed environment often signals trouble. It can mean the organization has evolved as far as it is going to and is on its way downhill. On the other hand, clutter, noise, and seeming confusion often are signs of growth. Case in point: Airports, with their need to handle rapid growth while continuing to serve the public, are constantly interlaced with scaffolding. The architect who could come up with an expandable airport would go down in history!

At a stopover at the Albuquerque, New Mexico airport during major remodeling in 1988, I got so caught up in their attempts to make an unavoidable situation tolerable that I nearly missed my connection. Those in charge were doing an excellent job. Cartoonlike signs explained, gave directions, apologized—and relieved what could have been a grim and frustrating situation. These captions aren't verbatim, but they'll give you the idea:

> "We know these are the same old chairs; please come back and sit with us in our new ones."

> "This is the back of the front of this sign."

> "Please don't complain about these telephones to the telephone company. They've already told us how much of an embarrassment the phones are to them too."

Whether growth demands or the nature of the workplace are creating the dirt, noise, and clutter, a creative mind can make conditions tolerable by adding a light-hearted note.

When unavoidable things happen, those who have a sense of humor bend like the proverbial willow; those who don't are likely to break like the proverbial mighty oak. Recently in Iowa I heard of a gas station that had been leveled by an explosion. Someone had placed a big sign out front with this message: "I said a Bud Light!" This, of course, is a reference to the Budweiser's Light beer commercials. Isn't it wonderful when people can keep their sense of humor in the face of adversity? To me, the sign also emphasized the value of using humor in advertising.

Humor can also alleviate monotony. Waiting in line is a fact of life, but I think the only people who could possibly enjoy it are those paid by others to stand in line. Can you think of anything more boring? I can't! A few years ago, when the World's Fair was held in Canada, one of the biggest complaints was that visitors had to stand in long, time-consuming lines to see the exhibits. The lines to the Disneyland exhibit were as long as the rest, but at least Disneyland provided entertainment for those waiting, turning a minus into a plus. Relieving boredom is one of the functions of the array of cartoon characters interacting with the crowds standing in line at Disneyland, Kings Dominion, and other theme parks.

Other organizations have used this idea as well. A New York bank features live piano music for customers standing in line. Elevators in an office building are surrounded with mirrors to make the wait seem shorter. What better way to entertain and relax people than to give them a reason for laughing?

On the other hand, in a workplace devoid of management humor, employees will create their own. Sometimes their humor will take the form of horseplay, goofing off, or counterproductive behavior.

"I sure feel like telling the boss where to get off again."

"What do you mean, again?"

"I felt like it yesterday too."

Strategies to relieve frustration or "put one over on the boss" rarely involve direct confrontation. I once worked at a public agency where the humorless executive director had a habit of opening and reading all mail addressed to employees, even mail marked "personal." Rather than confronting the boss, the employees began sending each other letters marked "personal," telling of espionage and romantic encounters. Then they would gather as the boss opened the mail and watch while he read such cryptic messages as "I finally got the secret plans from my government source. Meet me Monday under the bridge, and bring the money. Remember, it's to be $250,000 in small, unmarked bills!" This type of humor emerges as a natural stress-relief measure, in the same way that gallows humor emerges quite naturally and predictably in police work, combat, or other extremely high-stress jobs.

One group of employees I read about sent a bouquet of flowers to their boss's family. The accompanying note read: "You have our deepest sympathy. We only have to work with him; you have to live with him!"

This was rather a crude way to send such a message. A milder method of sending a humorous but critical observation was the case of the *seagull award*. The vice president of a large company would often fly in from corporate headquarters to inspect and make changes in the operations of the regional office. Upon his retirement, he was presented with a giant inflated plastic seagull. When he asked about the significance of the gift, he was told, "When you'd come in from headquarters for one of your quick visits, you were just like a seagull. You'd fly in, circle round, make a lot of noise, defecate on a few people, and fly off again!" Here was a case of sending a creative but belated message on the wings of humor.

When a work-related situation finally does get the better of you and you realize it is not going to improve, you might consider doing what I did. A consultant hired by the organization where I worked gave me good advice after acknowledging a demoralizing situation and its permanency there. He said, "Why don't you ask yourself how you can turn this situation to your advantage? For example, the CEO deals around you, which means you have time you otherwise wouldn't have. Why not use that time for other things that will advance your interests?" I decided to use the extra time to advance my speaking goals. The consultant's ability to look at the overall picture and put my situation into proper perspective helped me make my decision.

A technique used by many who become stressed out by a boss with whom they cannot communicate is to picture the cause of their distress in diapers or in horns and a tail. Forming humorous mental pictures of one's tormentor is a popular way of combating the stress associated with that individual.

Humor Reframes What You Say

Several years ago, a poll was taken in Switzerland wherein respondents were asked the question "Do you believe it is okay to smoke while praying?" An overwhelming 83 percent responded no. A similar group was asked the same question reframed as "Do you believe it is okay to pray while smoking?" The answer was just as overwhelming: 90 percent said yes.

The way something is worded can alter responses drastically. When a New York Times/CBS News poll asked people if they favored a constitutional amendment "prohibiting abortions," a majority opposed it. But when asked if they favored an amendment "protecting the life of the unborn child," over two hundred people switched sides.

Reframing in its simplest form can be seen in the use of euphemisms, where an inoffensive word or expression is exchanged for one considered offensive or blunt. What once were city dumps have become landfills. Or they may be referred to by a realtor who is trying to sell adjoining property as "bird sanctuaries." They look and smell the same, but the euphemism creates an image of filling land rather than dumping junk.

Airlines are prolific users of amusing reframing to increase profits. They've painted planes with smiley faces. Life preservers have become "personal flotation devices," and other expressions have been reframed to persuade customers that flying is fun.

American Airlines was losing money on its *red-eye flights*. They had a negative image, and people were not using them. First, American changed the name to the *Midnight Special*. Then extra attendants were put on the flights to ask for musical requests. They provided free music videos and free champagne, making the flight a party. American advertised the *Midnight Special* as a fun thing. Business increased by 70 percent.

When communicating with your work mates or customers, in writing or orally, reframe your language to make your requests and ideas more acceptable to your audience. Being able to think funny will enable you to reframe creatively. At a community college I know of, a planned class titled "The American Revolution and the War of 1812" was to be dropped for low enrollment. Its savvy instructor saved it by changing the name to "Thirteen-Star Wars and the British Empire Strikes Back." Humor also allows you to say things that would otherwise be either forbidden or extremely difficult to state in an acceptable way.

A woman in San Diego works with law school graduates to prepare them for the bar examination. She is not a law school professor. In fact, she probably knows no more than the average person about the law. What she understands is people and the concept that fun is fertile. She knows that we can get the best from people, including ourselves, if we like what we are doing. She knows that excellence is never achieved through perceived drudgery. So she takes these law school graduates and gets them to view the forthcoming law examination as they would a game of Trivia. She reframes the exam into a challenge that they learn to approach with positive anticipation. The pass rate of her group is substantially beyond that of the other examinees. Similarly, games like Authors are actually learning experiences reframed into games.

Humor Defuses Criticism and Hostility

One of the great advantages to thinking funny is the ability to confront awkward situations and present them in a humorous vein. This is the best way to defuse criticism.

When John F. Kennedy appointed his brother Attorney General of the United States, news reporters questioned whether his choice was appropriate. His answer: "I see nothing wrong with giving Robert some legal experience as Attorney General before he goes out to practice law."

Self-deprecating humor probably goes further toward defusing hostility than anything else. What are the dynamics at work in a hostile situation? Both parties are, naturally and understandably, on the defensive. If they aren't already in a closed mode, they soon move into one and set up their defenses. Now picture this: You are ready to be attacked, you are prepared for me to tell you that you are stupid or to otherwise defame you. But instead I make a disparaging remark about myself in a good-natured way. You are taken aback. Your options are to go ahead with the defensive harangue you've prepared and feel like a fool or to laugh with me. My guess is that you would at least rethink your position and give us a chance to settle things peacefully.

John Wayne, portrayer of heroes in dozens of movies, was considered by some a "big macho phoney." The criticism was leveled at *The Duke* because of his strong stance on military preparedness and his lifelong association with guns. The Harvard Lampoon dared him to appear in "the most hostile territory on earth" to defend his political and philosophical views. Surprisingly, Wayne accepted. In a frontal attack, he rode a tank from the airport to the campus, walked on stage carrying a toy rifle, and opened by announcing "Coming here is like being invited to lunch by the Borgias." His self-parodying humor defused students' criticism and hostility and got them to listen to and understand his point of view. At the end of the talk, the crowd stood and chanted, "Duke, Duke, Duke."

Of all the practical uses of humor, defusing tension and hostility is certainly one of the most valuable. You can see the dynamics at work in a physical demonstration. Make a tight fist with your left hand (if you're left-handed, use your right hand). Now, with your other hand, grasp the wrist below the fist, also very tightly. Now relax the fist. Did you notice that your grasp on the wrist automatically relaxed too? In hostile situations, self-deprecating humor works the same way as relaxing your fist. It draws the other person into the open mode, so both of you can be relaxed, open, receptive, friendly, and cordial. This principle has application in both interpersonal relationships and business situations.

San Diego's Horton Plaza is one of the inner city's proudest additions. It has been a smashing success, bringing hordes of shoppers downtown and millions of dollars to the many shops. However, a major difficulty has been an enormously confusing parking layout. Many shoppers have gotten lost for long periods. The promoters acknowledged this flaw by making fun of the parking situation when they unveiled a new directory system. They sent some two hundred invitations to the news media, complete with magnifying glasses, poking fun at the detective work needed to find one's way through the multileveled center.

Nowadays, not much can be covered up for very long. Companies, politicians, and individuals are admitting to errors and offering solutions before the public can confront them. They realize that it is usually easier to defuse criticism than it is to defend yourself after being criticized. So be prepared when a potential for criticism exists.

Eight

Setting the Stage for Productive Meetings

*If you have enough meetings over a long enough period of
time, the meetings become more important
than the problem they were intended to solve.*
— Henderickson's Law

*A modern business meeting is very much like a funeral,
in that you have a gathering of people wearing uncomfortable
clothing who'd rather be someplace else.
The difference is, a funeral is held for a specific purpose.
And when that purpose is accomplished, a funeral breaks up.
But a meeting goes on and on until the leg of the highest-
ranking member falls asleep.* — Dave Barry

I don't mean to dismiss or even downplay the importance of meetings. The results of a productive meeting resound throughout an organization. On the other hand, unnecessary, time-consuming, nonproductive meetings more often than not slow down or even halt progress.

*Meetings are like panda matings. The expectations always are high, but
the results usually are disappointing.*

41

Meetings are self-perpetuating and appear to have become our national pastime. According to those who meet to study the current state of meetings, 50 million meetings are held each day throughout the world (not counting the one you have to attend in about five minutes). Senior executives spend an average of seventeen hours a week *meeting*, plus six hours getting ready and four more recovering. Managers are being "meetinged" to death. Some executives ironically refer to the day's scheduled meetings as their "dance card." Yet, we are told, nearly all of those meetings are ineffective in accomplishing their purpose.

Theoretically, business meetings are held for one of two purposes: to disseminate information or to solve problems. In actuality, too often they end up serving as an arena for fighting turf battles while those who are not participating in the combat flinch and turn inward.

Many CEOs and managers believe that instituting a *brainstorming process* will turn meetings into forums for creative management. However, if the setting is too formal and a rigid structure prevails, open communications are inhibited and creativity is in fact stifled. More often than not, people are called into a meeting to share and receive information and then are put into the closed mode, which discourages sharing. How can they think imaginatively and use their creativity to solve some organizational problem when the closed mode has promoted tunnel vision and inhibited the flow of creative juices? The process is counterproductive.

Research shows that people who laugh together get almost twice as much done as those who do not.

A few years ago, the most popular theory making the rounds was transactional analysis (TA). The concept was originated by Dr. Eric Berne and presented to the public by Thomas A. Harris and Amy Bjork Harris in their *I'm O.K., You're O.K.* books. According to TA, everyone operates out of three basic ego states: parent, adult, and child. While in a parent state, we are critical, nurturing, and overprotective; in an adult state, we act intelligently and logically. But when we try our hand at problem solving, we need to bring alive the child state existing in all of us. At least in the initial stages, we want to stimulate the childlike attributes of curiosity, inventiveness, and freshness, seeing everything as new. The excitement and wonder that children typically have help us change old ways of thinking. Then we can come up with new ideas and different ways of looking at old problems.

In problem solving, perspective is everything. Humor generates perspective. It helps us stand back and see the issues clearly, which is a critical factor in assimilating new information and coming up with new approaches. Whether you are holding a meeting to pass along information or to solve problems, everyone will benefit if you establish an atmosphere of fun and encourage people to think in nonstandard ways. No one will volunteer information if they suspect you might "kill the messenger." However, if you remove the intimidation, they will open up and give you their solutions. By fostering the open mode, you will promote receptive minds and honest, forthright feedback. Then you will find that most problems can be solved in-house.

It is incredible how often questions can be answered by those involved when they are encouraged to offer solutions. The management of one of New York's leading museums was about to sign a contract for a costly study to find out which exhibits were most popular with visitors. Just before the contract was signed, a committee member suggested that they could get the information simply by asking the janitor where he had to mop the most.

One of my clients, the West Coast regional office of a Fortune 500 corporation, held a retreat at the famed Hotel del Coronado. The group had some problems to solve and decided they would brainstorm with their own staff members. Rather than spending money on an outside consultant, they hired an events specialist to help them put their own people in an open mode for the meeting. This company understood the importance of establishing a productive atmosphere. Planners surrounded the participants with upbeat posters of surfing and other seacoast activities. The kickoff was a steak fry on the oceanside esplanade so everyone could meet informally. Masquerading as a banking expert, I convinced the group that I had expertise in their field. Using background information that regional management had given me, I launched into a miniroast of their top people from the head office in New York. Thus the mode for the upcoming sessions was set. Old ideas of *big me/little you* were discarded.

The regional manager later told me that the meeting was a success and they found the solutions they had sought. He also joked about how pleased he was that his fellow workers had shared with the company the creativity they usually reserved for their expense accounts. He was certain they achieved positive results because they created a setting for open and productive sessions. At the same time, he recognized the importance of camaraderie and the ability of participants to laugh at themselves.

In direct contrast to that experience, my next speaking engagement was quite a letdown. I began to suspect my reception would be different when the manager who hired me asked me to wait outside during dinner. Of course, you can imagine how much my confidence was boosted when the same manager said he was afraid his boss would discover the surprise (me) prematurely and castigate him for it. While awaiting my cue, I overheard several of the attendees on their way to the restroom complaining about every aspect of the gathering. This did indeed turn out to be a very difficult audience to entertain and make laugh.

Those two experiences convinced me that a good barometer of how people feel about themselves and their teammates is their ability to laugh at themselves and laugh together. In other words, the health of any organization is directly proportional to its ability to laugh at itself.

Here's another formula: The number of people attending the meeting and the length of the meeting are inversely proportional to its usefulness. Usually too many people are meeting for too long in the wrong place at the wrong time in an unproductive atmosphere. Thus, in addition to introducing a liberal dose of humor, you might consider limiting participants to those directly affected by the subjects to be discussed and limiting any meeting to an hour. If your staff tends to be long-winded, you might consider borrowing an idea from ESSO (the forerunner of EXXON). When a speaker went over the allotted time, the lectern emitted smoke and animated cartoons were shown on a screen behind the speaker.

To get a meeting started in the right direction, consider telling participants up front that you would like their help in making the meeting productive and more enjoyable—by having fun. The promise of fun can take the dread out of both small and large meetings. This technique will work because it is based on human nature.

Energizing and Revitalizing Meetings

A Freudian slip? A memo slated for distribution read, "The next meeting of the committee will be in the administrative conference room. Please allow two dull hours for the meeting."

Meetings don't have to be dull. Try to look for different ways of bringing fun and play to every aspect of your meetings. A happy, productive frame of mind is the result whether you use subtle humor or out-and-out slapstick. With practice, you will discover what style best suits you.

Preestablish the mood of those who must attend your meeting by using humor in the announcement. Keep the meeting alive by bringing in props, planning a roast or put-on one of the more popular VIPs, using funny awards, or staging a cartoon contest. One CEO wore a camouflage helmet to a meeting and passed out hats for others to wear.

Some open each meeting with a joke. Try assigning that task on a revolving basis, with everyone taking a turn at supplying the upbeat opening. For those who do not customarily expose themselves to humor, this is an especially good exercise. For everyone else, the opening joke breaks tension, starts things on a positive note, and fosters the open mode necessary for a successful meeting.

Another tried-and-true tactic is to get a small trophy featuring a spark plug (available at most trophy stores for less than ten dollars) and award it to the person who *sparked* the meeting the most, the one most instrumental in bringing the meeting to life. At the next meeting, the recipient could award the spark plug trophy to someone else who meets the criterion. Similarly, a rubber chicken or a *turkey* award could be given to the one who came least prepared or detracted most from efforts to have a successful meeting. Variations of these *message* awards could be half a toilet seat, as used by a major insurance company, or a trophy featuring a horse's posterior. These awards add humor but also make an important point.

If you are distributing a pile of papers with the agenda, slip in a cartoon. Preferably it will relate to some aspect of the agenda, but an unrelated cartoon is better than none at all. If the meeting is a lengthy one, have a humor break midway through. A proponent of interjecting humor would say, "Go for the jocular vein instead of the jugular vein!"

Awards, Roasts, and Put-ons

I write and conduct comedy roasts as a regular part of my profession. I always approach them with caution, because roasts incorporate a special type of humor that must be handled carefully.

First, the targets of this type of chiding humor must feel very secure about themselves and feel O.K. about the foibles that will be exploited during the roast. Unless the roastee is having fun, the audience will not have fun. Thus I always ask the roastees and others who know them well about their sensitivities. In other words, what is off limits? The guest of honor at one roast was balding. I found out that he was particularly sensitive about his lack of hair and did not like to be kidded about it. In these cases, you work around the particular sensitivity. Sometimes, actually quite frequently, you find people who are unroastable because their dignity is too easily offended.

The other important dynamic of a roast (which provides some valuable lessons in the use of humor in general) is that those who do the roasting must have impeccable motives that are clear to their target.

Why not have an *honorary* roast at your next meeting? After all, what better way is there to demonstrate how much you love the boss than to gang up on him or her with some chiding humor? A roast is also a great way of paying tribute to someone who is retiring or leaving for another position. If done correctly, the honoree will cherish the roast forever. In fact, it is a good idea to tape the event and present the tape to the roastee for posterity.

An all-time classic roast must be carefully planned. First, the person to be roasted must meet certain criteria. He or she must be well liked, respected, and colorful, or at least a bit different in some ways. Most important, the roastee must be very self-confident.

Next, find out from the roastee and his or her acquaintances what is off limits. Leave out anything that would offend. If there are too many off-limits items or if the person lacks unusual characteristics, you will have trouble coming up with enough jokes for a full-blown roast.

The final step is to list the things making that person different and to then devise humorous ways of presenting the differences to an audience. Remember that a roast is a verbal caricature and therefore must involve some exaggeration.

Here is some material excerpted from a roast that the management team of a large aerospace company prepared for their director of procurement. Festivities began with some roast *openers*:

"There are only few times in our lives that we get a chance to honor a man of great intelligence, a man of wit and wisdom. Unfortunately, tonight is not one of those times. Instead, we are going to talk about Jerry."

"A great deal has been said about him. And I see he's here tonight to deny it."

"In all fairness, it should be said that he is a humble man. Of course, he has much to be humble about."

"A lot of people fought over who was going to be on the dais tonight. Those who won are, of course, not here."

"Ann Green wanted me to tell you that she really would have liked to be here this evening, but this is the night she paints her toenails."

As you can see, so far this is all general material that you could say about anybody. More specific comments by the roasters:

First Speaker: "I had to give up a lot to be here tonight—mostly my self-respect. Jerry is known for, among other things, his fame as a football player. (Jerry played pro football briefly for the Denver Broncos). I'm told that while in high school, Jerry earned two letters in sports. One told him not to come back to practice, and the other asked him to return the equipment. He went to college for two terms: Truman's and Eisenhower's."

Second Speaker: "Well, I don't know which college Jerry attended, but I understand he had a relative who went to Notre Dame whose hobbies were climbing ropes and ringing bells. What I do know about Jerry is that he was a war baby. His parents took one look at him and started fighting."

Third Speaker: "I'm proud to be a friend of Jerry's. And it's not easy being a man's only friend. We've been friends for many years, and there's nothing Jerry wouldn't do for me. And that's about what he's done for me—nothing. But I have to say that this is a man who, busy as he is, has always been able to find the time to listen to our problems, and then to add to them."

At the end, the roastee got some time for a rebuttal:

"I want to say that it's nice to be among friends. Even if they're not your own. Years from now, I'll sit down by the fireplace, pour myself a cognac, think about tonight, and upchuck. I do want to compliment the people who organized this affair. How they felt they could bring it off without speakers or material is beyond me! It's nice seeing Lowell up here. That is, what you can see of him (Lowell was a short fellow). He worked his way through college standing on wedding cakes."

In addition to providing you with some usable material should you decide to conduct one of these all-time classic comedy events, the above excerpts also demonstrate why everyone must like each other and be able to laugh at his or her own foibles. If it's done correctly, a roast can be one of the best ways to have fun while reinforcing relationships.

Meet Me in the "Meeting" Room

If your organization is large enough to have a special room for meetings, you might consider giving the room its own name. But don't do what my former employer did. I once worked in an organization where the chairman of the board was disliked by every manager except the CEO. When the chairman retired, the CEO named the main meeting room after him. Thereafter, announcements read "A meeting will be held tomorrow at 10 A.M. in the Hubert J. Scrooge (not his real name) Conference Room." What a way to prepare us for a positive and productive session! I usually sat in the meetings devising ways to occupy my mind until they ended. One of my exercises was to mentally add up the hourly rates of the managers involved in the meeting—to see the total amount of money that was being wasted.

Apple Computer used the same idea in a more positive way. There the meeting rooms are named by employees and follow the theme of the building. In one building, rooms are named after the characters in *The Wizard of Oz*.

In another, the seven meeting rooms are named after the seven deadly sins. What better place to meet to discuss increasing profits than in the Greed Room? Or the Lust Room for planning the Christmas party?

Keeping Creativity Alive

At one organization I was with, meetings began with the meeting leader, who served on a revolving basis, asking the question "What is the byword for today?" This question was answered by the same person each time. He would rise and, in a booming voice, yell, "En-thu-si-asm!"

My suggestions for incorporating humor into your business meetings are proven ones, but it is important that you come up with your own ideas tailored to your audience. The thing to remember is that what is fun to one person may be boring or frivolous to another. You might try sharing the task of injecting a liberal amount of humor and fun into the meeting. If nothing else, you will learn what works with your group.

Since finding enjoyment in the workplace is still a somewhat far-fetched concept, some might look on your efforts with suspicion. The more you are departing from the standard fare or from what they have come to expect, the longer it may take to establish this newer, healthier, and more productive atmosphere. But keep trying, because the results will be worth the effort.

Typically, the people who attend corporate meetings begin to copy one another's behavior. When this happens, each person shrivels to half the person he or she could be, and the corporation consequently shrivels to half the organization it could be. Soon everyone has the same opinion, a development that psychologists call groupthink. The euphoria surrounding groupthink leads people to conclusions that fly in the face of reality. It has been said that groupthink caused President Kennedy and his best and brightest advisers to believe that 1,400 exiled Cubans could invade their homeland and defeat Castro's army of 200,000 under impossible conditions. Instead, the result was the Bay of Pigs fiasco.

The fact that President Kennedy fell prey to groupthink underscores the difficulty in avoiding it and emphasizes the necessity of contrarian, creative thinking by both leaders and participants. Those in charge of meetings can be most effective if they reserve time for creative silliness, even in the most serious meetings. Otherwise—groupthink will set in!

In summary, whether you are holding a meeting for the purpose of communicating information or solving a problem, you must create the correct mind-set. The most productive meetings are those attended by people in a positive, open, communicative, participative, creative mode. So think funny.

Nine

Turning Stress into Positive Energy

Stress is not an event, it is a perception of an event!

Earlier in the evolution of the human race, when fierce animals were our ancestors' most dreaded enemies, cave people benefited from their internal fight-or-flight mechanism. When faced with danger, their systems would pump adrenaline and initiate a whole set of responses designed to facilitate life-saving actions. The heart rate and blood pressure increased, ensuring sufficient blood supply to the cells. The digestive processes shut down, and blood diverted to the muscles and the brain. Blood-clotting mechanisms were activated to protect against injury. The breathing rate increased to provide the blood with more oxygen, and the bloodstream itself was supplied with additional sugar and fats to provide fuel for quick energy. These responses prepared the body to either have a terrific battle or run away at top speed. The person who survived the emergency could then sit down, relax, and let all systems return to normal. Few of us will ever have to face a flesh-eating animal, but our bodies still react to stress in the same manner.

All organisms require some stress. One line of agricultural research is called "mechanically induced stress" (MIS). Studies done at Britain's National Vegetable Research Station have shown that cauliflower, lettuce, and celery plants that are subjected to torment grow up to be sturdier and more robust (though smaller) than those left alone.

Professional speakers and public performers also need a certain level of stress. Ask girls or boys, men or women, from kindergarten to retirement, what their reaction is to speaking in public. Before they answer verbally, their body language reveals their discomfort at just thinking about it. But professionals recognize and appreciate the adrenaline their bodies produce. Without some level of stress, their delivery would probably be flat. That rush coming from natural stress propels them onto the stage, giving them the energy to act with animation and to deliver their presentation with feeling. I've read quotes from Bob Hope and many other long-time performers saying that they still get "butterflies" before performances. However, they recognize the need for short bursts of stress and put the extra energy to use. The trick to handling butterflies is to get them to fly in formation.

Yes, some stress is good. We need it to function efficiently and effectively. The body's reaction to stress provides the energy needed for optimum performance. But stress should be of limited duration and properly relieved. Stress that is prolonged and unrelieved becomes distress.

A recent survey found that three-quarters of Americans now say their jobs cause stress. A poll among working women stated that 80 percent experienced stress in their workplace. For companies, the bottom line is lower productivity, increased absenteeism, and higher medical and worker's compensation costs. Some experts put the overall cost to the economy at $150 billion a year.

The prevalence of harmful, health-endangering stress is a relatively recent phenomenon. Until about 1950, stress was an engineering term used to describe a structural condition. What has happened during these past few decades? Experts say the culprit is change. Change is so rampant today that we have to run just to keep up with the status quo. If you question that statement, look at what's happened in the world during the past fifty years.

In the business world, acquisitions, mergers, and new international competitors arise faster than anyone can keep tabs on. Job insecurity is growing at a time when "creative credit" has gotten too many Americans over their heads in debt. Financial problems, dropping profits, unreasonable bosses, deadlines, personality conflicts—these things threaten us as surely as wild animals threatened the cave people. They give us plenty to worry about, as if we didn't have enough already. (Worry is the interest we pay on tomorrow's problems that never occur.)

Now that you have been exposed to the many benefits of humor, you should be able to think of something that can limit the duration of stress and properly relieve it: HUMOR!

The next time a grizzly bear is breathing down your neck, try this exercise: Stiffen up and grab the sides of your chair. Make your entire body rigid. Now, maintaining the rigidity, smile broadly and genuinely. You can't do both at the same time, can you? When you smile, you relax. To smile is to relieve stress and tension. Laughter, of course, is an extension of a smile and also relaxes you. Relaxed, your mind will put your problems into proper perspective and open up to all kinds of creative ways to solve them.

Most of the time I've been fortunate in working with and for people with a fairly good sense of humor. In one organization, when we were demoralized from being forced to deal with too many difficult people, we decided to create a "rogue's gallery" in our meeting room. A photograph or caricature of each tormentor was posted on the wall. Think of the possibilities for creating your own "gallery"!

I believe in turning a minus into a plus—stress into positive energy—anytime possible. I regularly engage in tomfoolery. For example, irreverent posters hung in unexpected places and changed often can reinvigorate a whole office and prevent stress. Public service and fundraising drives provide an endless supply of basic material. I like the poster that asks for donors of toes for the "toe bank." Another good one is the first aid poster showing the procedure for dealing with a choking victim in a restaurant, to which some unexpected steps were added:

1.   Find out what victim is choking on.

2.   Don't order that dish yourself.

3.   Force liquid down victim's throat. If victim is choking on fish or fowl, use chilled white wine-if on meat, use room-temperature red wine.

4.   When blockage comes up, victim should consult doctor—bystanders should consult dry cleaner.

As I look back, I realize that I have always used humor to relieve stress in whatever workplace I happened to be. In 1975, I was executive director of a nonprofit redevelopment corporation in Lansing Michigan. Most of the supporting funds for this organization came from the federal government. Then a law was passed that had the effect of prohibiting future federal funding of the organization. As we prepared to disband and pondered our futures, there was a lot of stress, as you can imagine. The entire staff was preparing resumes to send to prospective employers. One of the ways we dealt with our stress was to see who could write the funniest, most extravagant resume. My favorites were the ones in which I was teased good-naturedly. For example, under Hobbies some people listed "Cooking gourmet meals for the boss" and "Procuring attractive dates for the boss." The fact that these little jokes were coming from people who were unsure of what the future held for them boosted my spirits.

Fighting stress with humor will prolong and enrich my life. That is why I am constantly working to perfect my stress-fighting techniques. There are several very simple things we can do to relieve stress. One is to have an immediate, established method for putting things into perspective. If you're at all like I am, you have found yourself getting upset over situations that, on second thought, do not merit the flow of negative juices through your body. The solution is obvious: Stop sweating the small stuff! Becoming a paraplegic or being sent to prison unjustly would warrant a high level of concern. But getting cut off in traffic or finding a typo in an inner-office memo would not justify stressing out.

How does your mind learn to distinguish between the *small stuff* and the *big stuff?* My method was to develop a personal stress scale. Start by listing ten events that truly merit your becoming stressed, and rank them in order of importance from 10 (most stressful) to 1 (least stressful). On my list, becoming totally disabled rates a 10 and finding out that TV Guide is in error about a show I want to see rates a 1. You have to decide for yourself how much worry any stress initiator merits.

The next time you feel as if your emotions are getting out of hand, stop for a moment, rate the event against the items on your scale, and then decide how much energy you wish to allot it. This scale tactic works. I know, because I use it all the time to deal with stress in my own life.

STRESS SCALE

STRESS SCALE

10	BECOME PARAPLEGIC
9	UNJUSTLY IMPRISONED
8	LOSE ARM
7	LOSE JOB
6	MAJOR TRAFFIC ARREST
5	IRS AUDIT
4	CAR NEEDS REPAIRS
3	SLUMP: GOLF GAME
2	CUT OFF IN TRAFFIC
1	FAVORITE TV SHOW CANCELLED

10	
9	
8	
7	
6	
5	
4	
3	
2	
1	

Another simple and fun technique for reducing stress is to study the editorial cartoons when you read the daily newspaper. How does a cartoonist create humor out of a national or local frustration (stress)? Most editorial cartoons contain exaggeration, irony, or satire. For example, one insightful cartoonist recently addressed drug abuse, which is probably the saddest situation in America. Reminiscent of charts depicting the evolution of human beings, the cartoon showed a kneeling creature sniffing something on the ground; then a somewhat more human creature standing partially erect; then an erect man; and finally that human creature back in the kneeling position sniffing lines of cocaine. I know of no other way the message could have been made more eloquent than through this humorous irony.

You can do the same thing with the stressful, frustrating situations in your life. Try the *what if* tactic. In other words, take the situation to its ludicrous extreme. Then look at it with irony (the exact opposite of what would be expected). If it still isn't humorous, try satire or exaggeration. When you find the humor in your stressful situation, you will feel *on top of it*. Humor provides perspective because it allows this kind of detached view and examination of stressful situations.

With practice, you can learn to laugh in the face of stress, thus limiting its duration and relieving it. You will come to recognize that much stress is self-induced. What hurts is not the stressful event but rather our reaction to it.

Ten

Strengthening Your Communications with Humor

Humor is the lubricating oil of business.
It prevents friction and wins good will.

According to studies, top-level executives typically spend 94 percent of their day in communications-related activities; middle managers, 80 percent; and first-level managers, 70 percent. How do these numbers break down? About 53 percent of the time is spent in meetings, 16 percent on the telephone, 25 percent in dealing with written material and mail, and the rest of the time thinking about how to communicate.

What underlying purpose is present in all our efforts at communicating? What is your main reason for sending letters and memos or making oral presentations? Why is so much money spent by advertisers? How do you get those you are training to listen, learn, and accept new duties and new challenges? I believe the main objective of all communication is to persuade.

The most beneficial way of strengthening all of the skills necessary for communicating is to use humor. Your sense of humor and fun will effectively build rapport, grab and hold attention, help people relax, bridge gaps in understanding—and ultimately persuade!

Persuading with Humor

Persuasive messages convince recipients that they have reached their own conclusions or made their own decisions. When you can lead people to think that an idea is their own, they are more likely to buy, cooperate, work harder and longer, and be happy with their decision to do so. Mark Twain gave us the classic example of persuasion in his fictional character Tom Sawyer, who got his fence whitewashed through the power of good-humored persuasion.

No one likes being told to do something as much as they like being asked to do it. Better yet, they like to think it was their idea in the first place. A little persuasive humor incorporated into most interactions with your work mates will lighten both your burdens and theirs.

Nowhere is humor more successful than in persuading consumers to buy products and services. For how many years have we watched that lonely, underworked Maytag repair technician and received his implied message? The conclusion reached by prospective buyers is that Maytag products are of such good quality they never need repairing, and a logical decision would be to buy a Maytag appliance. I'm certainly not saying that humor works every time with every viewer, but I believe a humorous, subtle message is much more persuasive than a talking head stating the facts and urging consumers to buy.

A good measure of a persuasive message's effectiveness is whether recipients retain it. For an example, let's look again at advertising. Advertisements would be worth very little to sponsors if consumers didn't remember the message long enough to get to a store and buy. One expert says that humor increases retention up to 800 percent. Of course, the degree of retention depends on a number of factors, including the relevancy of the humor to the point being made.

If you still doubt the power of humor to persuade, look at advertising in the mass media. It is estimated that two out of every three major advertising messages for major products employ an amusing or fun theme. To make this point in my talks, I usually provide the tag line from an old commercial or ad and ask the audience to tell me the name of the product. For example: "Sorry Charlie, only the best tuna get to be ..." At least half of the audience will shout out "Starkist." It's an old ad, but most people remember it because the theme involves humor. If you have any doubts about the power of advertising, remember that millions of us now believe yogurt tastes good!

There are several reasons for advertisers' shift to humorous, fun themes. Surveys tell ad agencies that people want to be entertained by ads rather than preached to or lectured. The average person, it is said, is bombarded by an estimated three hundred commercial messages daily. Of these, only about ten are retained in long-term memory.

We all have our favorites. A fast-food chain and a remedy for upset stomach gave America the punch lines for dozens of jokes: "Where's the beef?" and "I can't believe I ate the whole thing!" Neither commercial is recent—one was used over a decade ago—but chances are that you remember Wendy's and Alka Seltzer were the sponsors.

When intellect meets emotion in a contest to persuade, it is usually no contest. Emotion will win hands down. So never underestimate the power of humor as a persuader.

Humor Builds Rapport

Humor reaches out and puts its arm around the listener and says,
"I am one of you, I understand," and implicitly it promises,
"I will do something about your problems." —Robert Orben

One of the first things I learned in the speaking business is the importance of being liked and accepted by the audience. Rule #1 is if they don't like you, they will either spend their time silently disagreeing with your every statement or they will shut you out. Professional speakers have a saying about the importance of blending humor into a presentation: "You don't have to use humor in your talks; it's necessary only if you want to get paid." Successful clergy, business executives, club officers, motivators, and other types of persuaders will also tell you that they use humor to build rapport with their audiences.

Well-timed insertions of humor not only enable you to establish rapport with your audience, but they also help audience members establish rapport among themselves. First they smile with you and then with one another. They catch someone else's eye and say with a smile, We are enjoying this together.

Laughter is a highly valued form of audience participation in the speaking profession.

Whether you're standing in front of a huge crowd or in a line waiting for a cashier to get a price checked, a smile and a few good-humored words can establish rapport.

Besides establishing rapport within your workplace, humor builds emotional and intellectual relationships between your organization and the public. If customers or clients come in without a smile, give them one of yours. I know that is a cliche, but cliches have withstood the test of time. I like to use cliches in letters and memos as rapport builders. One of my favorites is "If at first you don't succeed, quit. There's no sense making a fool out of yourself." One variation is "If at first you don't succeed, you'll get plenty of advice." This idea has lots of application in the workplace, where things often don't go according to plan, and it can be tailored to cover a variety of situations. The point is that cliches make excellent little humorous blurbs to be sprinkled liberally throughout your correspondence.

You can use humor to maintain your own positive and upbeat attitude. One day in a supermarket I noticed that several bunches of green onions had slid to the floor. Since they had been lying on the floor, I hesitated to pile them back on the counter. I mentioned the onions to an employee walking through the department. "They're not mine. I don't start getting paid here for ten more minutes," he said, with a look that implied I should mind my own business. Here was an employee who could be counted on to waste time watching the clock and then be first to declare, "Thank God, it's Friday!" But instead of letting this employee's bad attitude affect me, I remembered the story of the big Texan who ambled into the vegetable section of the supermarket and told the clerk that he wanted to buy half a head of lettuce. The clerk told him they didn't sell halves of heads of lettuce, but the big Texan loudly insisted. Finally, the clerk went into the back room and said to his supervisor, "There's this big-mouthed Texan insisting on buying half a head of lettuce," at which point he noticed the Texan standing in the doorway. He finished his sentence by saying "and this gentleman would like to buy the other half."

I had a quite different experience when I recently stocked up on odds and ends at a hardware store. When I need anything they carry, I will return to that same store. What made it different? Not prices; they were competitive. Not convenience; there are at least half a dozen similar stores nearby. The deciding factor was the good-humored service I received from the woman at the cash register. She didn't just remind me to pick up rebate slips and ring up items separately so I could have receipts to remit for the rebates; she smiled at me and at those waiting behind me for service throughout the transaction. I apologized to the other customers for taking so long. But the cashier established rapport among all of us with a smile and the statement "Hey, if it were me, I'd want to get the rebates too, wouldn't you?"

Humor Draws Attention

No matter how well thought out or well articulated your message is, you are wasting your time if you cannot attract your audience's attention. Renowned defense attorney Clarence Darrow gained much of his fame from stories circulated about his attention-getting tactics. In one case, the trial was coming to a close and the prosecutor rose to deliver a summation to the jury. As the prosecutor began speaking, Darrow lit a cigar, sat back, and listened politely. As he smoked his cigar, the ash grew, but Darrow didn't flick it off. It became very long and was obviously about to drop off any second. The jurors were captivated by the ever-lengthening ash and could not resist sneaking a look at it while the prosecutor argued on and on. By the time the prosecutor finished, nobody was listening; everyone was watching incredulously the six-inch cigar ash. The clever Mr. Darrow had inserted a wire up the middle of the cigar. Similar shenanigans made him famous.

Whatever your reason for facing an audience, whether it is a single person or a crowd, you will benefit by integrating attention getters into your message. Ask questions, show benefits, and interweave relevant and subtle humorous material in a manner that will keep both you and your audience interested. The point is that there is no communication unless the parties are paying attention.

Humor Relaxes

Anyone who has observed a hypnotist or studied the techniques knows that about 85 percent of the process involves relaxing the subject and less than 15 percent involves implanting the message.

In your own communications, you need to send out subtle signals designed to relax whomever you are trying to reach. As you already know, humor relieves stress and helps people relax. When they're comfortable and they know you're comfortable, they can more easily absorb your message. The suggestions I offer throughout this book will directly or indirectly put your audience at ease and into a receptive mood.

Humor Bridges

As much as we hope for a time when "man's inhumanity to man" is no longer an issue, we all know that it does in fact exist. Properly applied humor works better than any other attitude to bridge the gaps. It's pretty hard for you not to like me if we're laughing together.

For anyone who tends to take himself or herself too seriously, a sense of humor should be number one on the list of desirable traits to develop.

A woman manager often is tested by the men she supervises to see how tough she really is—and if she can take a joke. If she can laugh but not tolerate shoddy work results, she can do well. The effective use of humor signifies confidence and self-assurance. The thing to remember is that, because of their upbringing, men usually are directing their resentment at "being bossed by a woman," not at the woman manager personally.

Eve Arden once handled a practical joke played by her leading man magnificently, in a manner that would not have occurred to a humorless woman. The phone on stage began ringing when no ringing was called for in the script. Arden could tell by her leading man's expression that he was in on the prank. Without missing a beat, she picked up the phone, said hello, listened a moment, then handed it to him and said, "It's for you."

Usually jokes, quips, or anecdotes about potentially touchy subjects are not appropriate, unless you know your audience well. But your sense of humor, whether you are on the giving or receiving end, will bridge many gaps. In nearly all cases, good humor will be met with good humor—a smile, a laugh, or a friendly retort. Respond to humor with facts and figures and you will be open to the charge that you can't take a joke or that you don't have a sense of humor.

In a room of fifty people, ask by a show of hands how many believe they have a sense of humor. I'll bet every hand will be raised. Of course, you'll see the people in the audience looking at one another as if to say, "What are you doing with your hand up? The last time you laughed was when the boss told her annual joke." But take for granted that they all do have a sense of humor and use it as an emotional bridge for working together.

Written Versus Oral Communications

Humor is equally applicable in communicating both orally and in writing. However, there are some differences in the way it's used. A joke may fit very well into an oral presentation of any appreciable length, for example, but it would take up too much room in a memo. Quips, quotes, amusing observations, and the like are more appropriate for your letters and memos.

Three things are important in incorporating humor into your communications: the lead-in or follow-up, relevance, and appropriateness.

Consider the following story, which could fit well into a variety of oral presentations. Everybody but Clyde had signed up for the new company pension plan, which called for an employee contribution. Unfortunately, 100 percent employee participation was required to put the plan into effect. Clyde's boss and his fellow employees pleaded with him without success. Finally, the company CEO called Clyde into his office and said, "Here's an enrollment form for the pension plan, and here's a pen. If you don't sign the form right now, you're fired." Clyde picked up the pen and signed the form immediately. "Now," said the CEO, "would you mind telling me why you couldn't have signed up earlier?" "Well sir," said Clyde, "nobody explained it to me quite so clearly before." This story touches on a number of issues, including persuasion, authority, and participation. If you told the story in a presentation involving a point about participation, you might want to follow up by saying "There is more than one way to get the participation you want." This remark reminds them why you told the story. Actually, you told the story to get a chuckle and insert some humor—but it also makes a relevant point.

For written correspondence, look for quips, quotes, and other humorous inserts. Quotes by well-known people are my favorites. They have the additional advantage of getting attention because of the famous name. A quote that could have been an excellent example in a couple of places in this book is one from Woody Allen. When asked what he wanted people to say about him a hundred years from now, he reportedly replied, "I'd like them to say, 'He looks good for his age!'" I've used this quote in more than one business letter. I've also used it enough on the platform to know that nearly everyone gets at least a chuckle out of it.

When I use the Woody Allen quote in letters, with his name in bold type so it jumps out at the reader, I follow up with "What your employees say—and even think—about your company is vital to its success." This comment is followed by a sales message about my program on making the workplace a pleasant and enjoyable environment. Another of my business letters closes with the same quote, followed by "I'm not looking that far ahead right now, but I am planning next year's speaking schedule, and I'd like to include you in it."

Humor in Correspondence

Consider these two letters:

Dear Mr. Smith:

This is to advise you that we are in receipt of your letter dated January 9, 1991, which concerns the shipment of widgets that you claim has not yet been received. At the present time, we are examining our . . . .

Dear Mr. Smith:

It was good to hear from you the other day, although I'm sure we both wish it could have been for a different reason. There is a slogan around here that says "Teamwork is important—it gives you someone to blame things on." I don't think you are interested in who is to blame but rather in how soon we can rectify this unfortunate delay. We've looked into it and expect to be able to send the widgets by tomorrow.

I hope you'll pardon the delay and accept our best wishes for the New Year.

Which letter would you rather receive or, for that matter, send? Letters should be warm, friendly, and conversational—written the way you speak, not as if you wrote them from the depths of a food freezer or swallowed a bureaucratic phrase book. The stilted, archaic way of writing memos, letters, manuals, and other business information should be relegated to the past, where it belongs. Perceptive business people tend to write in an informal manner and use humor. Humor is appropriate and effective in written messages for the same reasons it is appropriate and effective in oral communications.

Humor can by used to make nearly all of your messages more appetizing. But keep in mind when using humor that it is a spice, not a main ingredient. You have to use the right type in the right place and in the appropriate amount. Humor should enhance your point, not overwhelm or replace it.

Because I am an advocate of using humor as an attention grabber, I take special notice of letters I receive that employ the technique. Nobody likes being sent a form letter in response to an inquiry, but when the volume of mail makes a form answer necessary, humor can make it more palatable. For example, a letter I received started this way: "Congratulations! You now have in your possession an official, absolutely authentic, undeniably sort of helpful Form Letter Response to your incredibly well written and extremely intelligent inquiry. We regret this cold, impersonal form letter. However, because we receive tons of mail each day, a more personal response is impossible." I would have preferred a "customized" response, but the humorous flavor of this one made it more palatable.

Those in direct marketing frequently use humor in cover letters to both sweeten the message and get attention. Here's the humorous opening of a letter I received recently, which hooked me and led me into the sales message:

> In Sam Cypert's powerful new book, *Believe and Achieve*, AON Corporation CEO Patrick Ryan talks about Vince Lombardi's dedication to the basics: "Once, after the Packers had played a particularly bad game, Lombardi got on the bus, held up the ball, and said, 'Gentlemen, this is a football.' From the back of the bus, Max McGee spoke up and said, 'Coach, you are going to have to slow down; you're going too fast for us.'"

I am not suggesting the use of jokes unrelated to your subject—especially in written correspondence—but quips, quotes, and observations that provoke a smile energize your message and establish rapport between you and the recipient. The next time you write a letter, you might want to try one of the following openers:

> I recently read a contemporary axiom: "If at first you don't succeed, give up. Failure may be your thing!" I have tried, unsuccessfully, to reach you by phone, and rather than follow that adage, I decided to stick with the old one and "try again."

> There is an old Chinese saying: "A picture is worth a thousand words." A slide show provides both. Our meeting next Monday will feature a slide show about (whatever) that I think you'll find entertaining.

These kinds of openings soften up readers, get their attention, make the message more palatable, and verify your friendliness and goodwill—all without detracting from the seriousness of the point.

When I have tried and failed repeatedly to get a message acknowledged, one of my favorite tactics is to send a humorous telegram. How many people do you know who would ignore a telegram? So far, I haven't found one, and this method has never failed to work. That's probably because a telegram packs a one-two punch: an attention-getting communique with a good-natured, palatable, and rapport-building message.

I do not believe it is possible to overstate the power of humor in getting the attention needed to sell your message. Humor-studded tactics are often the only way to get through to hard-to-see prospects. One salesperson made a prospect the beneficiary of the huge sum of flight insurance available at all airports. Sending it to the prospect, she wrote on the policy, "My last thoughts were of you." Another salesperson sent a homing pigeon with this message: "If you want to learn more about our company, throw our representative out the window." I mentioned these ploys in one of my presentations, and at the end a salesperson came forward with another one of her own. She said she often removes the arm of a doll and sends it to an elusive prospect with this message: "I'd give my right arm to see you!"

When I hear about such ingenuity, I can't help believing that both the sales representatives and their prospects benefit from such good-natured messages. Whether your memos are designed to chide, invite solutions to problems, or prepare open mind sets for meetings, they can benefit from a humorous touch. A humorous message doesn't take any longer to write but is more effective, so why not try one?

Humor in Oral Presentations.

Nowhere is humor more necessary than in oral presentations. It not only moves the talk along, enlivens it, and invites attentive listening, but nowadays it is expected.

Nearly everyone recognizes the need for humor in presentations, but most people are reluctant to use it. Why? Because it involves risk. What happens when you make an attempt at humor and nobody laughs? Will you look foolish? Will you need to apologize? It could happen. But that small risk should never be a reason for not using humor. People who make even feeble attempts at using humor are seen as more personable than those who don't, and there are ways of minimizing risk.

I always carry with me—in memory—a joke, the humor of which I find especially lingering. I use it to put me into the open mode when I want to slip into it quickly. I also use it to "think funny" and get a surge of confidence at times when I need it, like when I get up to speak. Before getting up to perform (and all good presentations are performances), a speaker should exercise—the same way a diver would do breathing exercises before diving into deep water. My exercise is some humorous imagery and this remark by President Kennedy: "I'm healthy, I'm happy, and I'm here for fun." Then I go on with gusto.

A good manager must learn to speak effectively in front of an audience. In effective short presentations and full-blown speeches alike, the key ingredient is humor. It hooks the audience, holds them, and makes them go away remembering what you said—three crucial aspects of selling yourself and your message. At the end, the audience should leave in a good mood. They will remember you and what you said much, much longer if you've helped them laugh or at least smile a little.

Notice that I said the key ingredient in effective speaking is humor, not jokes. Andy Rooney is thought to be one of the most humorous guys in America today. That's why he has appeared for years on 60 Minutes, a highly rated TV show. People smile all the way through his dissertations, but nobody laughs wildly. Mr. Rooney seems to strike us as being amusing more than hilarious. This is all you are seeking to be.

It is especially dangerous to equate inserting humor with telling an irrelevant joke. Whatever humor you use must sound as though it is part of the speech or presentation. Jokes prefaced by "This is really going to make you laugh" or "I heard the funniest story the other day" will trigger the skeptical response "Oh yeah? This better be good!" Your joke will elicit little more than a polite "ha ha" or, more likely, groans.

If you do have a favorite joke and would like to fit it in, you can sometimes subtly introduce a subtopic that relates to the joke, then use it and return smoothly to your main subject. The quote by Woody Allen that I mentioned earlier could be used in relation to several subtopics: When asked what he wanted people to say about him (reputation) a hundred years from now (the future), he reportedly replied, "I'd like them to say, 'He looks good (appearance) for his age (longevity)!'"

If you follow all my good advice and still don't get the reaction you expect, you can always just move on as though you hadn't meant your story to be funny in the first place. But whatever you do, you really shouldn't worry if every attempt doesn't get the reaction you expect. Professional comedians and humorists think they are doing well if they get good responses to half their efforts.

Just in case your attempt to insert humor does not get the response you are hoping for, have some *savers* ready. The master of the *saver* is Johnny Carson. He uses timely, untested humor, and some of it is bound to fizzle or get a groan. When it does, he might say, "You'll get that one on the way home," or "Say bingo if I get to one you like," or "A little humor there—very little." Be on the lookout for *savers* you like. Select three and commit them to memory; you will feel comfortable knowing that, no matter what the audience's response, you are covered. And don't be surprised if your *saver* gets a bigger laugh than the joke.

Quips, quotes, and observations are throwaway lines and don't require saving. If they don't get a response, just go on as if you weren't expecting any. Save your *savers* for full-scale jokes that might fall flat. The term "return on investment," used in financial circles, also applies to joke telling. The longer the joke, the funnier the audience expects it to be and the more they expect to laugh.

One way to decrease the risk of telling jokes is to try them out on close friends or associates to see what kind of reaction you get. If your joke or story goes over well with them (and you should be able to distinguish between genuine amusement and a courtesy laugh), there is no reason it shouldn't go over well with a less familiar audience—as long as the two audiences share certain commonalities. Five basic variables influence a person's perception of what is funny: gender, age, education, culture, and language. There are things that I find hilarious when few others do. Those who do share my sense of humor usually have similar personalities or have many of the five variables in common.

The setting also determines what is funny. The audience response to a joke about flatulence will be totally different in a comedy club than it will be in a boardroom.

It will not take many speeches for you to be able to sense when your audience's sensibilities are threatened by a joke. Or when their attention is dwindling. When they do seem to be losing interest, it's time to blend in some humor. No matter how interesting your topic may be, your audience may start drifting, sometimes never to be regained, without occasional mental exercise.

Humor in Training

Much has been written about people being either "right-brained" or "left-brained." "Whole-brain communication" results when we use humor to relay our messages. The left brain absorbs the technical data being communicated, and the right brain is stimulated by the emotional impact of humor. Messages delivered on the wings of humor are received better and remembered longer. Research shows that laughing people learn more.

Training is a challenge in the sense that you are asking the trainee to take on new duties or learn new skills. Thus risk is inherent in the training process.

You can increase the challenge if you decrease the risk. Imagine an acrobat devising and perfecting acts without using a safety net. How risky would the new feats be without something underneath to cushion falls while the acrobat practices? Humor gives the trainee a safety net that takes away the fear of attempting new or greater challenges. It signals the goodwill of the trainer and invites trainees into an open mode, where failure can be accepted.

Remember that permission to fail is permission to grow. Growth is not possible without failure—that's how we learn. Can you imagine teaching a baby to walk by slapping it when it falls down? People undergoing training need to know it's okay to fail temporarily in the learning process. If they believe such failure will meet with authoritarian disapproval, they will be tense, rigid, and guarded—all features of the closed mode—and will be deprived of the opportunity to learn from their mistakes.

Suppose you're conducting a training session on doing a specific task. If you involve trainees and get them to laugh at counterproductive behavior, you reinforce their learning experience. The correct way will be embedded in their minds in a way that cannot be duplicated with any other method, not even explaining over and over and over.

Humor at the beginning of your training session can put trainees into a receptive mood. Gather humorous stories about your own and others' mistakes while attempting to learn the new skill or take on the new responsibilities. Stories like these will not only invite trainees into the open mode but will also let them know that failure in the pursuit of learning is expected and accepted. Relating your own mistakes or failures is an excellent way of making that point. It is a persuasive way of indirectly saying "I have failed before in the process of learning, so I expect that you'll fail in the process as well, and that will be okay!"

For nearly twenty years, I designed and managed urban revitalization programs for cities across the country. One of the tricks in doing this was being able to work with the various socioeconomic groups involved in the effort. Rebuilding the inner-city brings together bankers to loan the necessary money, state and local government officials under whose control the programs come, real estate and construction professionals who implement reconstruction, and those whose lives are directly affected by the changes. I was viewed with suspicion by all of them.

When I arrived in one major city, I found that the staff had recently been keelhauled before the city council and much maligned in a negative newspaper series. If that weren't enough, they all were on layoff pending my redesign of the program. You can well imagine the prickly atmosphere that prevailed when we met. To a person, they were on the defensive, wondering who I was and what was going to happen to them.

At our first session, I opened by saying that I wanted to discuss an affliction I had. It was one, I assured them, that they would recognize because they themselves had been, from time to time, temporarily sidelined with it. I then reverently placed in front of them a large poster showing a guy bent over in a strangely contorted position. I announced that I was, of course, referring to "cranial rectal inversion." They all broke up. Having gotten their attention and established rapport, I was able to begin the session. Early on they learned that, if I was taking anything seriously, it was the work that needed to be done. I told them a little about my background and assured them I wasn't on a witch hunt, that I recognized the difficulties of their task, that we would start from that point to rebuild the organization, and that all present would have a chance to prove themselves. In the first year with a challenge to do their best, we increased efficiency and achieved a production rate of 600 percent over that of previous years.

Whether you are asking participants to accept changes, take on new duties, or learn new skills, use a "humor break" if your training session is to be a long one or introduces a great deal of new data. After participants find out what the session is about, ask them to complete this sentence: "(Fill in your name) cannot do (whatever the session involves) because (a silly excuse)." You may learn a lot from the exercise, and the trainees will be having fun. The exercise has the effect of reinforcing all the reasons it can indeed be done.

Such humor techniques as exaggeration, irony, and satire are effective for nailing down your points during the actual training discussion. At a sales training meeting, for example, you could do a humorous skit about a really negative sales effort. Choose a trainee to act as a customer. Use statements like "You don't want to buy this, do you?" and "Would you be interested in buying this today, or would you like to think about it for a few months?"

Or you might tell trainees this story of *your* early beginnings in sales: "In spite of a good training program and a motivating sales manager, I lacked confidence in my ability to sell. One evening, while going over my appointments for the next day, I said to my manager, 'This is a very tough customer, and I don't think I can sell him.' Obviously upset, he said to me, 'What? After all the training I've given you, after I've taught you about the importance of a positive attitude, you stand there and tell me you don't think you can sell this guy! That's a negative attitude! For heaven's sake, man, be positive!' So I said, 'All right, all right—I'm positive I can't sell him!.'" The story can be adapted to fit whatever activity you are teaching. Later, if your trainees are tempted to embark on behavior like the negativity you parodied, they would very likely remember the story and stop themselves.

Suppose you were training salespeople in customer relations. A humorous skit that exaggerates poor service could advance their training enormously. Perhaps the skit could include a customer returning a sweater that was monogrammed incorrectly. The salesperson, instead of offering to immediately correct the mistake, could ask, "Would you consider changing your name?" Recalling laughs like these from their training might give the salespeople a safety valve when dealing with difficult customers.

You also could use a story that underlines the importance of positive mental attitude (PMA). Tell them about your neighbor: "The other night when I came home, I met my neighbor, who told me that a robbery had taken place at a nearby convenience store. He related that the clerk was shot three times. When I asked him if the wounds were fatal, he said, 'One of them was, but the other two were harmless flesh wounds.'"

Laughing listeners learn more. Perhaps you've been on an airline recently that uses humor to get across what must be the most ignored message in this country today: the safety message delivered at the beginning of every flight. Attendants on some airlines, apparently aware of their passengers' indifference, are injecting humor into the otherwise dry message: "Please don't smoke in the bathrooms, or you'll lose your bathroom privileges and will be asked to leave the plane at once," or "If we lose cabin pressure, an oxygen mask will drop out of the panel above your head. If you are traveling with an infant or someone acting like one, or a particularly slow business partner, put on your mask before helping them." Asked if he wasn't treating the safety message flippantly, an airline spokesman replied, "We try to maintain a fine balance between being humorous and still communicating the serious information in such a manner that people will listen instead of automatically thinking 'Here comes the recorded message.'" It is their way of being serious without being solemn. So the next time you're on a flight with one of the more astute attendants, on landing you might hear something like "Modern science has once again triumphed over fear and superstition. Now, will passengers please remain in your seats so that the plane gets to the gate before you do." The point is, whether you are involved in training, an oral presentation, advertising, or whatever—a message that is not heard is a message not received. Laughing listeners hear and learn more.

Making Your Point—Humorously

Don't we all tend to listen more closely to and accept more readily information we want to hear? Pleasant, funny, profitable messages are palatable and easily digested. So anytime it is possible, take the bitterness or unpleasantness out of your words.

How you phrase something is critical to the reception it gets. Sugar-coating messages in humor makes them easier to swallow. Everything can't be presweetened; an announced layoff, for example, would be difficult and probably inappropriate to joke about. But if you can learn to "think funny," you'll find you have the ability to make any message less distasteful.

Woody Allen, for example, declaring himself "appalled beyond measure" by Israel's treatment of rioting Palestinians, said, "My goodness! Are these the people whose money I used to steal from those little blue and white cans after collecting funds for a Jewish homeland?" Can you see how he used ironic humor to convey his dismay?

I recently noted the comment of one U.S. senator in reference to what he deemed an inconsistent position by another senator on a piece of legislation: "If I didn't like the senator, I'd say he's being deceptive. But I do like him, so I'll just say he's waffling."

In his book *How to Win Arguments*, William Rusher relates a story about his friend and colleague, William Buckley. As host of the television series "Firing Line," Buckley traveled from New York to Florida every weekend.

He would fly on Eastern Airlines and eat dinner en route. He especially enjoyed a couple of glasses of wine with his airborne meal. Suddenly the airline stopped serving wine on flights of less than three hours. Buckley changed airlines, and on each flight henceforth, he wrote a note to the CEO of Eastern, telling him how much he was enjoying his wine on the competing airline. This campaign not only resulted in a change of policy at Eastern but also netted Buckley a basket of fine wines from its chairman.

Instead of a No Parking sign, one business posted a sign that read "If there isn't a big, green, heavy truck here now, there will be shortly." No Parking signs with added impact read "Don't even think about parking here!" The person who made up this warning sign also had a sense of humor: "Thirty days hath September, April, June, November, and anyone going over thirty miles per hour." These signs make their point without sacrificing any of their seriousness. They are no less believable because they are packaged in humor, yet the public agency that posted them conveys goodwill and a good nature.

Eleven

Developing Your Humor Style

*To be happy ourselves is a most effectual contribution
to the happiness of others.* —Sir John Lubbock

*A sense of humor is an attitude, and attitudes can be learned.
Old ones can be changed, and new ones can be developed.*

Perhaps you are committed to making your workplace more enjoyable—or perhaps you're undecided whether this idea of having fun at work is for you. You may be thinking, quite naturally, "I don't want to make a fool of myself, and I wonder if familiarity with my employees might threaten my authority and diminish their respect for me."

I wrote earlier in this book about the importance of giving people permission to be themselves. I didn't mention that the first person to whom you must give this freedom is yourself. A leader without a sense of humor is like the lawn mower at the cemetery: He has lots of people under him, but nobody is paying him any attention.

Let me remind you that we are talking about job satisfaction through enjoyment of the environment. I am not suggesting that you come into work tomorrow with a lampshade on your head, carrying a rubber chicken or doing comedy routines—unless that happens to be your style. I am suggesting that you and your management staff sit down together and talk about how you, as a group, can make your workplace more pleasant and how all the employees can have more fun performing their tasks.

You may be able to save your sanity by cultivating a sense of humor, but you will need others' cooperation and enthusiasm to make an enjoyable workplace a reality. It is important to remember that you are not responsible for providing all the humor; only for putting up the green light that will allow it to flourish. You might begin by announcing that you would like employees to enjoy coming to work and then create a committee to work out how that can best be done. Then you can work on enhancing your own sense of humor and contributing to and benefiting from, like everyone else, the regular doses of laughter.

Nobody is born with a sense of humor. If yours is well developed, chances are you come from a home, education, or work environment that encouraged laughter. Or maybe you've learned from the school of life to sharpen your "fun" skills. If you've gotten this far in your life and think you can see nothing amusing about anything and that you probably never will, if after trying the exercises in the next few pages you still feel you have no sense of humor, run, don't walk, to a professional who can help you find why you are missing one of the best reasons for living—the sharing of laughter.

Advice from one of the most successful actors of all times might be relevant for those of you who are making your first attempt at developing a personal style of humor. Cary Grant, when asked about his secret for success, told the interviewer that he looked for someone he truly admired and then pretended to be that person. Modeling is a very effective way of developing almost any skill.

I once had a speech coach who explained to me the finer points of the term "influence." We often read or hear that a certain painter, sculptor, or other artist or performer was influenced by another. The coach told me that what this usually means is one has copied another's work, adapting it and adding to it until it has become a personal style. You and I don't have to feel uncomfortable about emulating the style of someone we admire either. Our own personality will modify whatever we use to encourage fun and laughter in the workplace, and it will become unmistakably ours.

Very little humor is original, so don't hesitate borrowing a line here and there. Anyway, imitation (or is it immigration?) is the sincerest form of flattery. Abraham Lincoln was a notorious appropriator of other people's stories, which he quoted as though they were his own. When confronted by a journalist who accused him of plagiarism, he admitted it, saying "I'm a performer, not a playwright!" I don't mind attributing material to the person from whom it was borrowed.

In the world of professional speaking, we have a method of adopting another speaker's quote. The first time we use it, we precede it with "As Sam Kaputnik says . . ." The second time we use the quote, we say, "As I once heard another speaker say . . ." The third time we use the material, we say, "As I've always said . . ."

Being Sincere

> *The key to success is sincerity. Once you learn*
> *to fake that, everything else is a cinch.*

I can think of very few things more annoying, diminishing, and frustrating than trying to talk with someone who is not listening. Even if the person is nodding and going through the motions of listening, I still can recognize when the lights are on but nobody is home.

Too many people in powerful positions have cultivated the appearance of being interested in someone even when they are not. For example, some years ago I patronized a small bank where the president often stood in the lobby shaking hands and smiling at customers. At first I was impressed with the man's friendly attitude. Soon, however, I realized that he wasn't looking at me; before I could answer his "How are you?" his eye was already on someone else. It didn't matter how I responded, he'd pat my shoulder and say, "That's great." One day, when he asked how I was, I smiled and said, "I'm terminally ill." He patted me on the shoulder and said, "That's great."

Perhaps that was the learning experience I needed to make me realize the importance of sincerity. Without a sincere interest in people, your sense of humor will remain underdeveloped. Step outside your own needs, try to see other viewpoints, and then you will start bringing it all together. It isn't enough to say "Our policy is to be friendly;" you must put that policy into practice.

I'm sure that lesson was driven home for one teller at a bank with the policy of being *friendly* with customers. One day a customer came into the bank to cash a check. On returning to his car, he realized that he needed his parking ticket validated. When he asked the teller for this advertised service, the teller said that getting a check cashed didn't merit a validation. Whereupon the customer wrote another check and handed it to the teller. It was for over a million dollars, and it closed out his account with that bank. As you can see, a set policy without sincerity is more than useless.

Taking Charge

Be honest with yourself: Are you open to change and improvement? I think you are. Otherwise, why in the world have you practically finished this whole book on the importance of humor? Once you've embraced the idea that everyone benefits from having a sense of humor and have accepted the necessity of being sincerely interested in others, you will have no trouble opening lines of communication.

The way you enter a room or welcome others sets the mood for the following interactions. If you look depressed or angry when you greet people or walk into an office, you can bet everyone else will be influenced by your example. But if you appear happy, enthusiastic, and interested, you will set a mood that ensures good communication.

Always give yourself a moment to study your audience, whether it is one person or a crowd. If they seem to be in a closed mode, take charge of putting them into an open mode. Unless you do, your time and theirs will be wasted. The relaxation, openness, informality, spontaneity, receptiveness, humor, fun, and play that you reflect will be mirrored by your audience.

Analyzing Your Humor Style

If you already have a well-developed sense of humor, you may still need to know how to translate your personal humor to on-the-job humor. Appearing not to take a task seriously is, of course, inappropriate in work settings. A little forethought is usually all that is needed to determine what is appropriate.

Keep in mind that the emphasis is on fun, with the notion that humor is certainly one of the best ways to promote fun. But both humor and fun are a matter of personal preference. I play tennis for fun. You may dance, play golf, hunt, or swim. I like chiding humor (roasting), but you may be turned off by that type of jocularity. Many intelligent people I meet enjoy puns. (By the way, puns are considered the lowest form of humor—unless they are your own. Puns more often elicit groans than get laughs. No matter; if they bring you enjoyment, then by all means have puns.) There is subtle humor, direct humor, racy humor, and insult humor. Few people like all types. But truly healthy people enjoy watching others have fun. Fun begets fun.

That is one reason I have not suggested that you take responsibility for providing all or even most of the humor and fun—just that you encourage it. As the leader, you must put up the green light for everyone to relax and enjoy work. You must also take your turn at instigating fun along with everybody else. It will not be enough for you to pay lip service to the idea; you must demonstrate by your behavior and participation that you are committed to the concept.

During humorless hiatuses, it's time for you to jump in and provide a boost. The sudden, unexplained absence of fun is a sign that something is wrong. Perhaps some obscure problem is gnawing away at your work team. Or perhaps some humor has misfired. In any case, it's always to your advantage to know about looming problems.

When you take responsibility for energizing the workplace, you will receive the added benefit of being able to ferret out problems. Humor is a good tool for delving. You could open a meeting with the story about the fellow going through a divorce trial. On the stand, he explains that every evening when he came from work he found a strange man hiding in his bedroom closet. His attorney asks, "And did this cause you great anxiety and anguish?" "Yes," answers the man, "I had no place to hang my coat!" You could then say to your work mates, "Folks, I feel like that man. Am I also missing something here?"

If you are hesitant about starting to express your sense of humor, you may first want to become a "closet humorist." Leave pennies in pay phone tills for people to find and visualize their reactions. If you're stuck in a traffic jam, say hello to and smile at ten drivers. Read cartoons and humorous cards until you find the ones that make you laugh. (Columnist Earl Wilson says, "Get well cards have become so humorous, if you don't get sick, you're missing half the fun.") Write your own autobiography using the most colorful words you can think of to describe your sense of humor, such as droll, zany, bizarre, cynical, corny, witty, insulting. Choose a couple of words that you feel best describe your humor style and recall several examples of when you reacted drolly, zanily, and so on. Or think of what you find funny in people you admire. These exercises will help you identify your style of humor.

Give yourself permission to start slowly. Begin by exposing yourself to humor and thinking about it. Venture out only as far as you are comfortable. Becoming humorous is like taking that first swim of the season: big toe first, then up to the ankle, the thigh, and when comfortable dive in!

Cultivating Charisma

Although we usually know it when we see it, charisma has always been difficult to describe and harder to achieve. It is a personal magnetism that creates a climate enabling one to put one's ideas and plans into effect. That is, of course, the very essence of leadership as well. Charismatic leaders are good communicators, they create rapport with those they need to reach, and they have a well-developed sense of humor. They encourage us to continually reach for better things. And yet charismatic leaders almost always joke about things that need to be put into proper perspective—including themselves. Self-deprecating humor comes easily to them. As your appreciation of humor (your own and others') increases, so will your charisma.

Recently, as the airplane prepared to back out of its stall on a flight to one of my speaking engagements, the pilot came on the P.A. system and announced, "Would the flight attendant please step out of the aisle so I can see to back up. That's a really small window back there!" Then, as we were deplaning, he said, "Have a great stay in San Jose." (We were in Palm Springs.) His sense of humor made the passengers feel good about both him (sight unseen, you'd probably invite him to your party) and the airline. And make no mistake about it, companies can have charismatic "personalities," just as people can.

President John F. Kennedy introduced a whole generation to the power of charisma. When asked what they liked about him, many Americans said that, although he was rich, he still understood the average person's problems and wasn't above laughing at himself. During his campaign for the presidency, aware that some would criticize the amount of money he had available, he announced at a banquet that he had received a telegram from his father: "Dear Jack," he read, "Don't buy a single vote more than necessary. I'll be damned if I'm going to pay for a landslide." At a dinner following his election, he said, "When we got into office, the thing that surprised me most was to find that things were just as bad as we'd been saying they were." Kennedy could also turn his good-natured humor against others. When Senator Barry Goldwater sent him a photo he had taken of the President and asked him to autograph it, the photo was returned with the following inscription: "For Barry Goldwater, whom I urge to follow the career for which he has shown so much talent—photography. From his friend, John Kennedy." (Kennedy inadvertently predicted Goldwater's subsequent awards for his excellent photographic portrayal of Arizona.) Kennedy's wit, used effectively throughout his presidency, was an essential part of his charisma.

President Ronald Reagan also used humor in his own charismatic style, kidding about his age, his memory, and his Hollywood background. One of the all-time classics in the effective use of humor was Reagan's second debate with his opponent, Senator Walter Mondale, in 1984. It generally was agreed that Reagan had lost the first debate. He had seemed confused and disoriented and was considered vulnerable on the issue of his advanced age and possible senility. During the second debate, Reagan was asked whether he thought age ought to be an issue in the campaign. His response will be long remembered and most revered by those of us who advocate the use of humor. He replied, "Well, I am not going to make age an issue in this campaign. I am not going to exploit for political purposes my opponent's youth and inexperience." For all intents and purposes, the debate was over, with Reagan the winner by an unexpected knockout. Why? Because Mondale could not top the remark.

First Lady Nancy Reagan, criticized for spending a little too extravagantly to please the American public, was accused of wanting to be "queen of the United States." She displayed a sense of humor by saying that she didn't want to be a queen because a tiara would mess up her hairdo.

When running for the presidency in 1988, George Bush both acknowledged his apparent lack of charisma and began acquiring some by stating in his nomination speech that he would try to keep his charisma in check. It should be noted that both he and his opponent, Michael Dukakis, had access to the best public relations and speech writing professionals. Bush used his resources effectively, But Dukakis came across solemnly in the media. One got elected, one did not. If you ever have doubted the importance of humor, this political example should help convince you; I'm sure it was a profound lesson for Mr. Dukakis.

If you want to develop your leadership skills more fully and acquire that magic trait called charisma, collect a repertoire of humorous remarks to use at appropriate times. Don't get caught without a quick-witted rejoinder. And don't worry about being spontaneous. Very few "ad libs" are created spontaneously; nearly all are extracted from one's memory bank.

> How I would love to be quick with a quip,
> fast with the answer that's clever and flip.
> But the witty retort much to my sorrow,
> pops up in my mind the day after tomorrow.

Your sense of humor will keep you mentally flexible, so you won't easily be knocked off balance. And it will attract people to you. You may never be a Kennedy or a Lincoln, but you certainly can develop some charisma!

Enhancing Your Sense of Humor

With some exposure, you will gravitate toward the kind of humor you feel most comfortable using, and of utmost importance, you'll begin to learn how to think funny. Once you identify what strikes you as amusing, you can begin to focus on that method of seeing the humorous side of almost any situation. Remember, all humor is based on the human condition. You might not find *black humor* funny. But if you were suddenly thrust into the highly stressful role of those who do, in all likelihood you would too. There is a rule in comedy: In order to make something funny to others, you must think it's funny yourself.

When you find something funny, share it with a friend. Put yourself in an accelerated program of humor sharing. Remember, humor is like love. If you would have it, you must give it away. Besides, the best way to hear new jokes (any joke is "new" if you haven't heard it before) is to tell others the jokes you hear and appreciate.

This principle is true with all humor. Make it a practice to seek out lots of cartoons. Not only will they teach you to think funny, but many can be converted to nonpictorial humor.

When you see a funny cartoon, tear it out and send it to someone you think will also appreciate it. If, for example, you see one involving an attorney, tear it out and send it to an attorney friend who would find it funny too. Do this with all occupations, hobbies, interests, and so on. When possible, personalize the cartoon by inserting your friend's name or initials. Personalized cartoons are more comical in the same way that oral jokes are more humorous if personalized. The receiver will get more from the joke or cartoon because of being involved in it. This humor-sharing technique is also an effective way of saying "I was thinking about you!"

Decide which subjects are best aimed at yourself. Never belittle your abilities, but use self-aimed humor to help others identify with you and recognize that you and they suffer from the same human condition.

Quite naturally, you will move toward the kind of humor that is your style as you expand your exposure to humor. But remember the AT & T rule: Humor should be Appropriate, Timely, & Tasteful. With such a variety of ways to express humor, you will lose nothing by leaving inappropriate humor out of the workplace.

Using Self-Deprecating Humor

Humor is a great leveler, because people can identify with those who can laugh at themselves. Thus humor is a must for the powerful. A contemporary sage remarked, "If you need to tell people that you are powerful, you are not." If you have power within your organization, people there not only are very much aware of it but most likely are intimidated by it. Self-directed humor, when used by the powerful, calls out to those who would be intimidated and says, "Hey, look here, I don't have such an exaggerated sense of importance about myself that I can't make fun of me and that you can't laugh at my expense." Such humor enhances rather than diminishes their leadership position.

To put self-deprecating humor to work for you, start by turning some *safe* personal foibles into subtle humor. For example, the *hair-impaired* have a lot of options. There may be a man somewhere who doesn't mind the loss of his hair, and there may be a place where no one will ever tease him, but I doubt it. I've heard quips like "I have the latest haircut—the one with a hole in the middle" and "I save my hormones for something that's more fun than growing hair." A medal should be awarded to the first man who, after having his smooth pate rubbed by a work mate and being told "This feels like my wife's behind," responded by feeling his head and saying "You're right, it really does."

Buddy Hackett, Roseanne Barr, John Candy, and many others have turned their weight into tons of money. One popular comedienne has built a hilariously funny routine around her cerebral palsy. Her hands shaking, she says, "I wanted to be a brain surgeon, but they wouldn't let me. So now I'm working in a restaurant—they like the way I toss a salad." Another comedian who seems to have no chin explains that he can't make his bed because he has no place to hold his pillow. Bob Ueker, a mediocre baseball player, built upon his mediocrity to become a television personality. All these people capitalized on what to most would have been a handicap.

So that your intentions are not misunderstood, it is important that all your self-aimed remarks be presented with a smile and in a humorous manner. Otherwise, people may think you are being cynical or seeing yourself in a negative way. You may even *manage upward* by admitting to a mistake before it is pointed out to you by your boss or board of directors. You could introduce your explanation with a quip like "I understand the other day my management skills were being compared to Lee Iacocca's—unfavorably, of course!" That kind of remark defuses the situation, injects some healthy good humor, and transmits your self-confidence in an acceptable way.

If there is room for any confusion following your humorous remark, be sure to signal your humorous intent. A big smile will help make the meaning clear. When anyone doubts whether you are being cynical or good-natured, your smile will be the deciding factor.

Helpful Humor Hints

Here are a few miscellaneous suggestions for becoming more humorous:

> If you have space, set aside a humor room or at least a humor corner. Keep a jar of colored jelly beans in it, with a list of what color to "take" for different stress situations.

> Put up posters in unexpected places. Change locations and posters often.

> If your group has to meet a deadline, ask for a present (for any holiday, including your birthday) of a specific job being finished or a product being developed on time.

> If faced with a problem, ask your workers, "How would Pee Wee Herman handle this?" To put them in a positive mood, say, "Now whatever you do, don't laugh."

> If you know your salespeople are giving their best but having a hard time selling the product, commiserate with them by saying something like "It sounds like our clients are getting rewards for finding faults."

When you suspect that those over you, or under you, have reason to criticize, take the initiative and put their feelings into a joke or a humorous, self deprecating remark. For example, suppose you missed an appointment or a scheduled meeting. You might say something like "I don't know how I could have forgotten. It's just got to be that I'm getting old. You know what they say: The second thing to go is your mind."

When possible, deliver first-time warnings with chiding (notice I didn't say "cutting"?) humor. Suppose you have an employee who never seems to be in her office. With a good-natured grin, you might say, "Jenny, does that '9 to 5' sign on your door mean those are the hours you're in, or are they the odds you set on my finding you there?" Unless Jenny is insecure or doesn't like you, this kind of humor will be received in the spirit in which it was intended.

THINK FUNNY! No matter what the situation, even if you have to turn it inside out and upside down, and even if you have to keep your insight to yourself, don't ever let a situation get the better of you. When you begin to see humor in your own behavior, you will have it made!

How to Tell a Joke

Your goal is not to become a comedian or even a humorist (although you may find that your success with humor will lead you to that) but merely to use humor and other forms of fun to nurture relationships and make the workplace more productive. Nevertheless, you will certainly be called on to tell an occasional joke. Some people can tell a joke, and others cannot. If you're one of those who cannot, don't despair. Those who get laughs every time have learned the dynamics of joke telling.

There is a story about a new prisoner who, on his first call to mess, noticed his fellow inmates getting up and stating a number. Every number caused the others to laugh. The new prisoner asked the guy next to him why everybody was laughing and was told, "Well, in here we've heard all the jokes. So we just give them a number, and the joke teller is recalling a particular joke." The next time the new prisoner went to the mess hall, he jumped up and said, "1." Nobody laughed. He got up again and said, "18, 43." Still nobody laughed. He sat down and asked his buddy why no one laughed. His buddy said, "Some people can tell 'em and some people can't!"

In studying what makes a good joke teller, I've learned a valuable lesson. When someone starts telling a joke you've already heard, don't interrupt to say you've heard it. Instead, pay attention to how the person tells it. Since you won't be waiting for the punch line (you already know it), you can concentrate on what the successful joke teller does. Did the person slide into the joke, or was the lead-in clumsy? Did the joke teller build tension and conflict in the best possible way? Were lots of excessive, unnecessary words included? How did the person deal with the punch line (was it crisp?) and the punch word? Was the joke set up properly with word pictures that created images on your mental screen? Analyze all this and incorporate the lessons, and you will become almost professional in your joke telling. (Another tip: Don't use dialect unless you do it really well!)

With practice and a little technique, anyone can become adept at joke telling. Just remember that all prepared, preplanned humor is most effective when it relates to what is being presented at the time and is not noticeably inserted.

Several things make a joke funny. First, people find things funny in proportion to the extent to which they can identify with them. A joke about golf is funnier to a golf player than to someone who neither knows nor cares about the game. Second, jokes aren't funny if they are inappropriate to the situation. Obviously, a church function is no place for a risque joke, but it would be appreciated and probably expected at a bowling banquet. Third, if a joke can be personalized, it will go over well. It's funnier to talk about you and someone who is present walking down the street, for example, than to talk about two nameless people. If you add that touch of realism, many will laugh without realizing they've just been told a preplanned joke. Fourth, if your joke involves characters, as most jokes do, give them so much life and color that your audience can see them in their mind's eye.

Every joke has three parts: a set-up, a punch line, and a punch word. In setting up a joke, use the above guidelines. Getting ready to deliver the punch line is very much like blowing up a balloon. You must to be able to sense the exact point at which you should let it explode. The more you blow up what comedy writers refer to as the joke balloon, the more tension you create—and the sharper and quicker the puncturing instrument, the louder the noise! Thus you must be careful to build the correct amount of tension and conflict. Polish a joke by looking for and throwing out nonessential words. The idea is to create the picture in the other person's mind.

Every joke has a punch line, and the punch line is always the sentence at the end of the joke. It completes the joke and, if told correctly, evokes laughter—or at least a smile.

Every punch line contains a punch word, the word that makes the joke work. Just analyze a few jokes, and you'll be able to determine the punch word. Many times it is the last word of the joke. Placing the punch word as close to the end as possible is critical to the success of your joke. Before you deliver the punch line, pause, alter your voice, and emphasize the punch word.

When you find a joke you like, quickly analyze it to see if it is set up right. Then look at the punch line, which should be punchy, and find the punch word. Is it as close to the end as it can be? If the joke has flaws, see if you can fix them. With a little practice, you'll be telling jokes like a pro.

How to Build a Personal Humor File

Once in a while humor is natural and spontaneous. But don't always count on it. In fact, much of what appears to be spontaneous occurs because someone has created a mental or actual file of adaptable humor. A personal file will benefit you in at least two ways: It will give you a reservoir to draw from, and it will make you think funny.

Thinking funny means developing *comic vision*, which will allow you to see the humor in events and situations. Alan Alda, one of the actors, writers, and directors of the television series "M.A.S.H.," said, "We had a seriousness of purpose. We also believed the old saying that to be serious doesn't mean to be solemn. We reveled in our lack of solemnity." In the best and worst circumstances, your comic vision will serve you well.

I have found that stories about my own funny experiences are the ones that others seem to enjoy most. Probably that's because being told about others' failures gives us hope. I remember when an older friend of mine was getting married. He invited me to the ceremony and the reception. I was not very well versed in the social graces, to say the least, but I knew you were supposed to take a present to the reception. Without a second thought, I bought my friend a shirt. Can you imagine the couple's reaction when they opened the box? Thank goodness I didn't realize back then what a social blunder I had made, or I might have been traumatized for life. To this day, that incident comes to mind each time I attend a wedding reception and see a table full of gifts. This little story has bridged many a gap with a younger person embarrassed by a social error.

"I can relate to that" may become one of your most used phrases when developing your own humor file. If you're always dieting, tardy, easily angered, messy, clumsy, or whatever, you won't be able to read a comic strip, read an article, or see a movie or television show without saying "I can relate to that!"

Using index cards or a computer program, make a file of jokes, cartoons, quips, quotes, anecdotes, observations, sayings, and everything else that tickles your fancy. For easy access, file each selection by what you believe to be its main point, then cross-index by subtopics. For instance, I would file Woody Allen's quote about wanting people to say a hundred years from now that he looks good for his age under the main heading of "reputation." You'll be surprised how quickly your file will grow into a voluminous collection of humor and how much fun you'll have developing it.

One special category in my file is a collection of quips for point makers and openings for business letters:

> Dracula is a pain in the neck, but . . .

> Picasso doesn't see things in perspective either.

> Speed kills. But around here, it merely astonishes.

> Idleness is tough because you get no rest periods.

In a matter of minutes, I can gather as many of these little remarks as I need for a presentation or business letter.

An excellent place to find humor is in joke books or books of humorous quips, quotes, and observations. But do not try to read these books as you would others. Spend only about seven to ten minutes at a time scanning for humor. Otherwise, you lose your perspective and overlook the merits of much of the material. I begin my day by reading for about seven minutes from a book of humor. I put my time to good use and get to start my day on a positive note, with a smile and fully in the open mode.

Twelve

Action Plan

Humor is contagious;
but don't wait to catch it from others;
be a carrier!

Before developing a plan for incorporating humor and fun into your workplace, you will need to examine present policies and ask yourself if they reflect light or darkness; if they are stretching or contracting employees; if they are constructive or destructive. The policies that are profitable and productive should be retained, but even they will be strengthened by your addition of fun, humor, and enjoyment.

Depending on the scope of your authority, you might be unable to initiate drastic or immediate changes. Or once you start making your workplace more enjoyable, you might become so creative that you'll be able to add pages to my *action plan*.

If you adapt the following suggestions to your personal situation, I believe you and your work mates will experience a new surge in job satisfaction.

1. Hire employees who show a capacity for enjoyment. You don't necessarily want someone who spends the entire work period telling jokes. Nor should you ignore such considerations as suitability and

qualifications. However, you should select employees who are predisposed to experiencing work as enjoyable.

2.   Clearly signal your employees that you would like to make the workplace more genial by injecting more fun into the daily activities. Be sure your managers are behind you on this. If applicable, it is a good idea to meet first with top management to go over your plans.

3.   Don't take all responsibility for creating this environment—just for getting permission to do it. Spread responsibility for implementation throughout the organization. Be sure to find ways of rewarding those who do the most to provide the fun and laughter.

4.   Find out what your employees consider enjoyable that can be used at work. One employee may find time and space for camaraderie appealing; another may find the opportunity for time alone attractive. The best suggestions for making a job more satisfying and enjoyable will come from properly approached employees.

5.   Designate a humor room. The ideal place is your break room. If your workplace does not have one, or if the break room is inappropriate as a humor room, create a humor wall or kiosk somewhere on the premises. The designated area can be used by employees to post sayings, cartoons, caricatures, jokes, and other funny items. Everyone should be encouraged to contribute. The employees themselves will not only help fill up the space but will also demonstrate what they consider to be humorous.

6.   Create a system to keep the idea alive, which is more difficult than getting it started. Your permission and the practice of having fun will provide impetus, but fresh ideas and novel ways to maintain a pleasant workplace will keep it going. Be sure you are an active participant; playing good-natured and appropriate jokes, contributing to the humor space, and becoming a frequent visitor are essential in keeping it going.

7.   Have at least one humor program a year—on an official holiday or a holiday you create. Bring in a humorous speaker or conduct a

comedy roast to honor one of the more popular employees. Or have a surprise birthday party honoring everybody who has a belly button.

8. Be sure your communications—both oral and written—include humor.

9. Always take a quick glance at your humor file before attending a meeting. Even if you don't have the opportunity to inject humor into the proceedings, being able to recall a few jokes may keep you from being bored to death.

10. Decorate your own office with an appropriate amount of humor. You might frame and hang your award for completing the second grade. Or if you have more serious credentials on your wall, consider placing among them a framed warranty for your lawn mower, vacuum cleaner, or other appliance. This will give you a sense of perspective about your credentials. It's also fun to watch how long it takes for someone to spot the incongruity.

11. Post humorous signs that carry either frivolous messages or serious (not solemn) ones. To comment on the overall organizational environment, post a sign that says "The squeaky wheel usually gets replaced." To convey a meaningful message related to your management objectives, post a sign that says "When you call upon a thoroughbred, he gives you all the speed, strength of heart, and sinew in him; when you call upon a jackass, he brays and kicks." A sign that says "Don't think of me as the boss; think of me as a friend who's always right," sends a message also.

12. Create personalized cartoons. If you see a picture in a newspaper or magazine, think about how it could be turned into a cartoon relating to someone or something at your workplace. Then caption and post it. Personalizing will add greatly to its humorous nature. Recently I was on a radio talk show. As I waited in the break room for the gentleman who was to interview me, I noticed these kinds of cartoons on the wall. Although I didn't know the individuals referred to, they were hilarious. One was a photograph of a woman

beating a man who was lying on the ground. This was captioned in journalistic style and named the woman as one of the radio station's salespeople. The caption explained that she was teaching a course at the local community college and demonstrating *tactful sales techniques.* Another photo was of a small child looking at a skeleton. The caption referred to the skeleton as the most successful participant in one of the local weight reduction programs and went on to say that the person had a few more pounds to lose but was hopeful about making the goal.

13. Create an organizational scrapbook. This same radio station had such a scrapbook in the waiting room, containing pictures of various parties at the station. Some were costume parties, which are humorous in themselves. All the photos had been doctored with humorous utterances along the lines of a comic strip. Ironically, the first question the interviewer asked me when we got on the air was how one puts humor in the workplace. He seemed genuinely surprised when I began to point out these examples from his own organization. I guess this story makes the point that humor can become an integral part of the work environment—in fact, so much so that the process becomes invisible and only the good results remain.

Try the above suggestions, but by no means be limited by them. Experiment with novel ideas; have an annual funny hat contest, as one of my clients does. Remember, you are limited only by your imagination.

Conclusion

The focus of this book has been humor. Please remember that humor, as we're discussing it here, is not an end unto itself. Of all the many wonderful things that happen when we laugh, probably the most important is relaxation.

It is very difficult to overstate the importance of relaxation, especially in the face of adversity or challenge. Only when we relax are our mental faculties at their best; only then can we think on our feet. But the physical part of relaxation is just as important. It is hard to imagine any activity that doesn't require a certain level of relaxation. In sports, athletes perform at their optimum level when they have reached a level of mental relaxation known as the Ideal Performance State (IPS).

Students in medical school are taught that a severed main artery spells death for the patient in three minutes. They are taught that the artery can be successfully reconnected in three minutes—IF THEY DON'T HURRY.

Relaxation is critical to almost any stressful task. This is evident to me every time I go onto the platform to speak. If I don't relax, the audience won't either. The mere act of smiling relaxes and gives confidence to the smiler—and relaxes the audience too. Try it. Put a big smile on your face and see how much more confident it makes you feel. That's one reason to smile when you approach any task.

Have you wondered why audiences are frequently warmed up by comedians? Humor is used to get the audience ready because laughing stimulates other emotions. After being stimulated by laughter, people are more responsive to other stimuli, including sex. That should get your attention! But it's true.

Rule #6. There is a story about a high government official who directed much of the war effort for Britain during World War I. Subordinates would come into his office continually, waving documents, emphasizing the high priority of this and the top secrecy of that. He would listen patiently and then tell them to leave the papers on his desk. As they neared the door, he would call out: "Oh, one thing." "Yes?" they would reply. "Remember Rule #6." "Yes sir!" Then, after a brief moment of thought, they would say, "Excuse me sir, but what is Rule #6?" To which he would answer, "Rule #6 is 'Don't take yourself too seriously.'" They would say, "Thank you sir. I'll remember that. But what are the other rules?" The official would then reply, "Young man, there are no other rules."

Will Rogers, the great humorist and philosopher, used to say, "We're only here for a short time. We need to learn to have a little fun and not take ourselves too seriously." That's good advice today, perhaps even more so in a time when stress is shortening so many lives.

Of course, humor in the workplace is much more than comic corollaries or humorous homilies. It is the experience of play, happiness, and good feelings. It is sharing the fun in funny and the joy in enjoyment. It is building work environments that are positive and productive. It is about harnessing the power of fun and laughter to get the best out of others as well as yourself.

Learning to have a better sense of humor will not only help you live longer and healthier, but it will help you be a better executive. Humor adds to executive skills. It enables you to get things done, as discussed in this book, but it is reflected in other attributes as well. Experts call attention to the similarity between joke telling, which is basically the yoking of two diverse and dissimilar things, and that much-prized managerial attribute, vision—which consists largely of seeing unexpected connections. Perhaps it is no coincidence that many of today's top CEOs, people like Lee Iacocca of Chrysler and Michael Eisner of Walt Disney Productions, are noted for their sense of humor and their ability to make the job fun.

TV personality Hugh Downs was said to be on the brink of giving up broadcasting as a profession. He found it demanding and had watched it drive several of his colleagues to drink and premature death. But after deciding to quit the business, Downs suddenly found that he didn't have to take it so seriously. Then he began to have fun. Says Downs, "I struggled with the business of broadcasting for at least a dozen years in dead seriousness. I made neither a name nor any money in it until I started having fun with it."

Should you be one who dismisses the importance of humor or finds no merit in the techniques and philosophies stated here, there is one additional thing I would like you to consider: the quality of your life. Please imagine for a moment that you have only a few hours to live. What would you do with that time? Would you kick the tires on your prized car? Or walk around your home admiring the grounds and architecture? Or begin counting your money? No. You would look to the intangibles of life: your family, your friends, the times you laughed and loved. These times would be connected with whatever humor you've allowed into your life. Even if you don't want to modify your management style, you'll be happy when the time comes to "check out" that you enhanced your sense of humor. And your loved ones will be happy from the moment you do start looking at things with a sense of humor.

Living life without a good sense of humor is like hauling a load of rocks down a bumpy road in a wagon with no springs. Humor is life's shock absorber.

May all your wrinkles be laugh lines.